TERRORISM,
U.S. STRATEGY,
and
REAGAN POLICIES

TERRORISM,
U.S. STRATEGY,
and
REAGAN POLICIES

Marc A. Celmer

Contributions in Political Science, Number 173

(G P)

Greenwood Press
New York • Westport, Connecticut

Library of Congress Cataloging-in-Publication Data

Celmer, Marc A., 1958-
  Terrorism, U.S. strategy, and Reagan policies.

  (Contributions in political science,
ISSN 0147-1066 ; no. 173)
  Bibliography: p.
  Includes index.
  1. Terrorism. 2. Terrorism—Prevention—
Government policy—United States. 3. United States—
Politics and government—1977-   . I. Title.
II. Series.
HV6431.C42   1987   363.3'2'0973   86-33647
ISBN 0-313-25632-2 (lib. bdg. : alk. paper)

British Library Cataloguing in Publication Data is available.

Library of Congress Catalog Card Number: 86-33647
ISBN: 0-313-25632-2
ISSN: 0147-1066

First published in 1987

Greenwood Press, Inc.
88 Post Road West, Westport, Connecticut 06881

Printed in the United States of America

The paper used in this book complies with the
Permanent Paper Standard issued by the National
Information Standards Organization (Z39.48-1984).

10 9 8 7 6 5 4 3 2 1

Contents

Charts

Preface

Terrorism—the word generates powerful images and feelings of fear and frustration. It is the frustration produced by the Iranian hostage crisis that sparked my interest in the study of terrorism. This work is the culmination of my studies.

In researching and writing this book, many obstacles were encountered. The chief one was the massive amount of literature available on this subject. Unfortunately, much of the literature, due to the rapid development and changing nature of the subject matter, becomes dated quickly. However, every effort has been made to present the most up-to-date material available.

How nations have responded to terrorism has been one of the most researched aspects of the terrorism issue. The major works in this area include Robert Kupperman's and Darrell Trent's *Terrorism: Threat, Reality, Response*; Ernest Evans' *Calling a Truce To Terror: The American Response to International Terrorism*; William Regis Farrell's *U.S. Government Response to Terrorism: In Search of an Effective Strategy*; and Alona E. Evan's and John F. Murphy's *Legal Aspects of International Terrorism*. All of these works add greatly to the body of literature in this area and represent some of the most comprehensive examinations of the U.S. response to terrorism. However, each work fails to present a complete picture of the U.S. response to international terrorism. Ernest Evans' work fails to discuss the governmental structure responsible for dealing with terrorism. William Regis Farrell's work fails to outline the U.S. use of international efforts to deter and prevent international terrorism. Although James B. Motley's work *US Strategy to Counter Domestic Political Terrorism* presents a constructive outline of the U.S. response to terrorism, he fails to consider steps taken by the Reagan administration to improve the U.S. response to terrorism.

Although the studies outlined represent some of the finest available, the best sources of data on U.S. policy are government documents, including Congressional hearings, official reports, and major policy speeches and statements. Government documents and interviews with government officials represent the primary source for this study.

Although I am responsible for any errors or omissions, this book would not have been possible without the help of numerous individuals. Foremost, I must thank Mr. and Mrs. James J. Foley and Stephen F. Celmer for their financial and emotional support. In addition, I would like to express my deepest appreciation to George Middleton, Kevin McConnell, Rosemary Reed, Joe Reap and Ambassador Anthony C. E. Quainton of the U.S. State Department and to Wolfgang Rosenberg of the U.S.

Energy Department for their assistance in answering my requests for information concerning U.S. policy; Tom Southall of American University's Computer Science Department for his assistance in tackling the problems associated with GMLThesis; to Russell McHugh, Nick Gilman and Maria DeMasi for their assistance in editing my manuscript; to Elizabeth A. Nichols, President, Wordflow Incorporated, and her staff for their fine effort in preparing my manuscript for publication; to my friends for their interest and enthusiasm; and especially to David Walsh, Professor of Political Science, Southern Connecticut State University; Paul Best, Chairman, Department of Political Science, Southern Connecticut State University; Duncan L. Clarke, Professor, School of International Service, American University; Larman C. Wilson, Professor, School of International Service, American University. Without their support this book would not have been completed.

1
Introduction: International Terrorism—
Issues and Questions

The nature of the international community has changed dramatically during the past 15 years. The time of U.S. hegemony over the international community's economic, military and political affairs has been replaced by a period of uncertainty and interdependence. American strategic nuclear superiority of the 1950s and 1960s has been replaced by strategic parity with the Soviet Union. The economic preeminence of the U.S. has been undermined by more competitive West European and Japanese products, by the steady outlay of billions of dollars in economic and military loans and grants to other nations and by a greater degree of interdependence and competition for strategic resources, mainly oil. Finally, U.S. political influence in world affairs has been adversely affected by the growing number of nation–states and non–state actors, symbolized by its reduced ability to influence the behavior of the members of the United Nations.

"The 1980s," as pointed out by William J. Taylor, Jr., and Steve A. Maaranen, "confront the U.S. with an increasing number and diversity of threats to its vital national interests."[1] One such threat is international terrorism, which has affected numerous aspects of international relations, travel and life. Few nations have been spared the effects of terrorism, with possibly the United States suffering the most. From 1968 to 1981, the international community witnessed 7,425 terrorist incidents that have resulted in 8,298 injuries and 3,841 deaths.[2] During the same period, American citizens and property were involved in more than 3,200 incidents, which annually represented between 35 to 45 percent of all recorded international terrorist incidents. The United Kingdom and Israel were consistently either the second or third most victimized nations, their involvement never exceeding 10 percent of all terrorist incidents.[3] Unfortunately, the mid–1980s witnessed an actual increase in the level of violence. In 1983 and 1984, 1,150 terrorist incidents were recorded.[4] An additional 800–plus incidents occurred in 1985 and approximately 350 in the first half of 1986.[5] This frightening escalation of terrorist violence, affecting mainly the Middle East, Europe and Latin America, has resulted, from January 1984 to May 1986, in more than 4,500 casualties, of which 1,500 were deaths.[6]

The issue of international terrorism is complex and perplexing. Amos A. Jordan and William J. Taylor, Jr., have termed it a "nontraditional security consideration,"[7] which, unfortunately, is not amenable to traditional diplomatic behavior.[8] An examination of some of the critical issues concerning international terrorism will be helpful in illustrating the numerous obstacles that have confronted the United States in its drive to combat international terrorism.

One of the most critical issues is whether there is any degree of consensus within both the international and academic communities concerning the cause, problem and nature of international terrorism. The international community has been divided over the causes of and thus the actions to take in dealing with international terrorism. United Nations Resolution 3034, adopted by the General Assembly on December 18, 1972, symbolizes the degree of division that exists within the international community over this issue.[9] The United States, the leader of the industrialized democracies, represents the status quo. It holds that any source of destabilization of the international environment is dangerous and must be dealt with. Algeria, on the other hand, represents the Third World and holds that political violence is a legitimate form of political behavior when peoples are confronted with injustice. Algeria and many other Third World regimes came to power through wars of national liberation—so, arguably, did we—and terrorist behavior. It is not surprising then for these nations to express their support for this form of political behavior. The best way to explain the difference in perceptions among nations is through the now classic and overused cliche "one man's freedom fighter is another man's terrorist."

The same clash of perceptions that affects the international community also affects scholars and the academic community. J. Bowyer Bell best stated the problem(s) affecting the academic community in his article "Trends on Terror: The Analysis of Political Violence." He stated that both the public and the academic response to terrorism has been historical, exaggerated and closely associated with congenial political postures: moreover, the academic perspective is conditioned by the nature of individual philosophy.[10]

This observation is supported by both the inability to formulate a consensus on a definition of *terrorism* and by the recent debate concerning the involvement of the Soviet Union in the so-called terror network. As pointed out by Alex P. Schmid and others, "there is no clear and generally accepted definition of what constitutes terrorism."[11] The international community, as illustrated above, is divided over the issue of terrorism and has failed to come to grips with it. The international community's attempts to deal with this issue is addressed in detail later in this book.

The academic community's approach to the subject of terrorism has produced no widely accepted guidelines for the study of this phenomenon. The issue of defining *terrorism* has in itself produced such a wide variety of definitions that classifying them has become a monumental task. Alex P. Schmid, in his book *Political Terrorism: A Research Guide to Concepts, Theories, Data Bases and Literature*, has compiled no less than 109 definitions, ranging from "Galtung's ultrabroad definition [to] Arendt's idiosyncratic definition."[12]

The election of Ronald Reagan has brought to the fore a debate concerning the Soviet Union's involvement in the occurrence of international terrorism. The first days of the Reagan administration witnessed public statements accusing the Soviet Union of directing the so-called international terrorist network. However, the Reagan administration's belief that the Soviets were the controllers of the present wave of international terrorism could not be supported by the U.S. intelligence community.

Despite the inaccuracy of the Reagan administration's statements, both the public and academic communities have taken up this issue. Through the Subcommittee on Security and Terrorism, the Judiciary Committee has attempted to compile evidence for the Reagan administration. However, the subcommittee's success has been questionable at best.

Ray Cline and Yonah Alexander have attempted, in their book *Terrorism: The Soviet Connection*, to prove a "persistent strategic pattern of international destabilization and terrorism assisted by, if not always controlled by, Moscow."[13]

The picture painted by Cline and Alexander and those who support their position resembles the cold war rhetoric of the 1950s. This position is contrasted with that of Walter Laqueur and, to a lesser extent, Robert Kupperman.

To those supporting the Reagan administration's position that international terrorism is a serious threat to the United States, Walter Laqueur contends that international terrorism is "an irritant, seldom if ever a real danger."[14] Robert Kupperman, in an interview with Laurence Gonzales, stated that "although Russia certainly provides funding for some terrorist operations, if it [the Soviet Union] withdraw that patronage, little would change. Terrorists know how to raise money. . . . there is really no need for a master conspiracy to keep terrorism going."[15]

The scope of the issues that are affected by international terrorism range from airport security to nuclear proliferation. There are no agreed–upon definitions, no accepted limits to the subject of international terrorism and no effective academic approach toward the subject. This situation most likely will not change in the near future.

In examining U.S. policy in combatting international terrorism, this book uses a historical, chronological approach sketching the causes, goals and organization of international terrorism. To illustrate the problems the United States faces in effectively dealing with international terrorism, only those terrorist events and groups that have a direct impact on U.S. policy are covered.

The Reagan administration, currently, is attempting to develop and promote a tough antiterrorist policy. On April 3, 1984, President Reagan signed National Security Decision Directive 138 (NSDD 138). NSDD 138 represents a decision in principle to use force against terrorism and calls for the greater use of covert actions and counterintelligence operations and the establishment of military and CIA hit teams designed to strike at international terrorists and their bases. The hypothesis being examined by this book is that the United States is inadequately prepared to execute the active self–help measures called for by NSDD 138.

This book is different from most other works concerned with the U.S. response to international terrorism because it examines more than one aspect of the U.S. antiterrorist program. It analyzes the various components of the American response to international terrorism, illustrating its strengths and weaknesses, and makes a current assessment. In addition, in order to present the most up–to–date and complete outline of the United States response to international terrorism the impact of the Iran–Contra Arms affair will be incorporated into this book. Despite the incomplete disclosure of the facts surrounding this affair, enough is known about the Iranian component of it. To avoid any confusion, the Iran–Contra Arms affair will be presented as the Iran arms–for–hostages affair.

NOTES

1. William J. Taylor, Jr., and Steve A. Maaranen, eds., *The Future of Conflict in the 1980s* (Lexington, Mass.: Lexington Books, 1982), p. 3.

2. U.S. Department of State, *Patterns of International Terrorism: 1981*, Department of State Bulletin (August 1982), pp. 9–11 passim.

3. Ibid., p. 14.

4. U.S. Department of State, *Combating International Terrorism*, Department of State Bulletin (June 1985), p. 73.

5. U.S. Department of State, *International Terrorism*, Department of State Bulletin (August 1986), p. 1.

6.   Ibid. The statistical data presented represents the most up–to–date available on terrorism as of February 1987. This has been confirmed by a telephone conversation with Joe Reap, Public Affairs Officer, Office for Counterterrorism, U.S. Department of State on February 6, 1987.

7.   Amos A. Jordan and William J. Taylor, Jr., *American National Security: Policy and Process* (Baltimore: The John Hopkins University Press, 1984), p. 555.

8.   John E. Karkashian, "Too Many Things Not Working," in *Diplomats and Terrorists: What Works, What Doesn't: A Symposium*, ed. Martin F. Herz (Washington, D.C.: Institute for the Study of Diplomacy, School of Foreign Service, Georgetown University, 1982), pp. 6–9 passim.

9.   U.S. Department of State, *U.S. Votes against General Assembly Resolution Calling for Study of Terrorism*, Department of State Bulletin (January 22, 1973), pp. 81–94 passim.

10.   J. Bowyer Bell, "Trends on Terror: The Analysis of Political Violence," *World Politics* 24 (April 1977): 476–488 passim.

11.   Alex P. Schmid, *Political Terrorism: A Research Guide to Concepts, Theories, Data Bases and Literature* (Amsterdam: SWIDOC, 1983), p. 1.

12.   Ibid., p. 13.

13.   Ray S. Cline and Yonah Alexander, *Terrorism: The Soviet Connection* (New York: Crane, Russak & Company, 1984), back cover.

14.   "It's an Irritant, but Not a Mortal Danger," *The Washington Post*, 29 April 1984, p. B8.

15.   Laurence Gonzales, "The Targeting of America: A Special Report on Terrorism," *Playboy* (May 1983): 171.

2
Contemporary International Terrorism

As pointed out in the introduction, one of the most complicated issues facing both the international and academic communities in dealing with international terrorism is the formulation of a generally accepted definition of *terrorism* and *international terrorism*. Theodore A. Couloumbis and James H. Wolfe defined a *terrorist* as a "nonstate actor employing standard and unorthodox forms of violence in pursuit of certain political objectives."[1] This definition is an accurate description of a terrorist; however, it lacks the precision and comprehension offered by Paul Wilkinson and Richard Shultz. Their definition recognizes four types of terrorism: war, revolutionary, state and sub-revolutionary terrorism. This book uses only the definitions of state, revolutionary and sub-revolutionary terrorism. *Revolutionary terrorism* is violence employed by revolutionary movements and groups as a means of "initiating a vicious cycle of terror and counter-terror that is intended to alienate popular support away from the target government," with the goal of bringing about political revolution and change.[2] *State* or *repressive terrorism* is "defined as the threat and/or employment of extranormal forms of political violence, in varying degrees, by an established political system, against both external and internal opposition."[3] As presented by Wilkinson and Shultz, this form of terrorism may be used "by an established political system against other nations and groups external to the particular political system, as well as internally to repress various forms of domestic opposition."[4] *Sub-revolutionary terrorism* is violence "committed for ideological or political motives but which is not part of a concerted campaign to capture control of the target state" and is used by anarchist or revolutionary groups to advertise their cause.[5]

International terrorism, like terrorism, is difficult to define. However, as a matter of consistency the following definition is used: "the threat or use of violence for political purposes when such actions are intended to influence the attitude and behavior of a target group other than its immediate victims and its ramifications transcend national boundaries."[6]

The above definitions are presented in a conscious effort to illustrate that there are different forms of terrorism. This fact has been obscured by the Reagan administration's attempts first to link the Soviet Union to the international terrorist network and then by its raid on Libya in response to suspected support by Colonel Khaddafi of the bombing of the La Belle disco in West Berlin in the spring of 1986.

A definition offered by the Department of State describes *terrorism* as "the threat or use of violence for political purposes by individuals or groups, whether acting for or in opposition to established governmental authorities, when such actions are intended to shock, stun or intimidate a target group wider than the immediate victims."[7] This definition, coupled with the department's definition of *international terrorism* as "terrorism conducted with the support of a foreign government or organization and/or directed against foreign nationals, institutions or governments,"[8] demonstrates the recent perception of terrorism as mainly a form of state behavior. There is no doubt that a number of regimes today aid and/or abet terrorism. But depending on your perception, any state action, carried out by either the United States, Libya or another nation, can be labeled as an act of terrorism. However, the need to recognize the reality that there are different forms of terrorism and that each is as dangerous as the next is paramount.

HISTORY

International terrorism is not a phenomenon unique to the 1970s and 1980s. Terrorism is a form of political behavior "as old as history."[9] The French Reign of Terror of the mid–1790s is viewed by some as the first serious use of terrorism in modern history.[10]

The 20th century has witnessed the evolution of terrorist behavior. The period from 1914 to 1940 witnessed two of the most significant international terrorist incidents ever. On June 28, 1914, Archduke Franz Ferdinand, heir to the Austro–Hungarian throne, and his wife were assassinated by a Serbian nationalist in Sarajevo, Bosnia.[11] The assassination of the Archduke set in motion a series of events that led to the outbreak of World War I. The second incident was the assassination of King Alexander of Yugoslavia. On October 9, 1934, King Alexander and French Foreign Minister Louis Barthou were assassinated in the streets of Marseilles, France, by members of the Ustasa–Internal Macedonian Revolutionary Organization (IMRO).[12] This incident led to the formulation and adoption by the League of Nations of the 1937 Convention for the Prevention and Punishment of Terrorism, the first international attempt at dealing with terrorism.

Terrorism in the first half of the 20th century was aimed at specific political targets. In contrast, international terrorist incidents of the 1970s and the 1980s have been aimed at a much wider spectrum of targets with little regard for or concern with injuries to innocent civilians. An illustration is the Lod Airport massacre. On May 30, 1972, three members of the Japanese Red Army, under contract to the Popular Front for the Liberation of Palestine, disembarked at Lod Airport, Tel Aviv–Israel, from Air France flight 132. Within minutes following the disembarkment of flight 132's passengers, the three Japanese terrorists opened fire with automatic weapons and hand grenades. This attack caused 28 deaths and 76 injuries.[13] The motivation for this attack was offered by Kozo Okamoto, the only surviving terrorist, at his trial. He stated that the attack was staged as "a means of propelling ourselves onto the world stage" and that the "slaughtering of human bodies is inevitable."[14]

CAUSES

One of the most complex questions challenging scholars and statesmen today is what causes individuals like Kozo Okamoto and groups like the Japanese Red Army to engage in such forms of political behavior. There are an estimated 400 terrorist organizations worldwide, not all of them active.[15] The difficulty in outlining the causes of terrorism is that each group, regardless of its political orientation, has its own unique motivations and goals. In the words of James Motley, "despite the polemical discussions and intellectual debates regarding terrorism, there is no single factor which is the universal cause of terrorism."[16] Nonetheless, Ted Robert Gurr's work in the area of relative deprivation and Samuel P. Huntington's work involving the process of modernization offer insightful examinations into the causes of terrorist behavior.

Gurr's work is based on the premise that "the potential for collective violence varies strongly with the intensity and scope of relative deprivation as actors' perception of discrepancy between their value expectations and their value capabilities."[17] The concept of relative deprivation is composed of three types of deprivation. The first is *decremental deprivation*, which occurs when "a group's value expectations remain relatively constant but value capabilities are perceived to decline."[18] The most-cited example of decremental deprivation producing terrorist behavior is associated with 1917 Russia and the huge loss of life and material produced by the battles of World War I. A more recent example is related to the defeat of the Arab nations, including the PLO, during the Six Day War of 1967. The Six Day War represented the Palestinians' last hope for establishing a homeland by conventional means. Brian M. Jenkins stated that "the Israeli defeat of the Arabs in 1967 caused the Palestinians to abandon their dependence on Arab military power and turn to terrorism."[19]

The second kind of deprivation is *aspirational*, which occurs when value "capabilities remain relatively static while [value] expectations increase or intensify."[20] The political violence occurring in many Third World nations today, such as in El Salvador, is rooted in aspirational deprivation.

The final example of deprivation is *progressive*. This occurs when "there is substantial and simultaneous increase in [value] expectations and decrease in [value] capabilities."[21] The 1956 Poznan workers' revolt in Poland is an illustration of the effects of progressive deprivation.

Samuel P. Huntington views the process of modernization as a means of ending the isolation of various ethnic groups. Although the breakdown of the polarization of a society along ethnic lines may be beneficial to social stability, the breakdown of the ethnic borders may also lead to some serious negative effects. As previously separated groups expose and compare their levels of wealth, power and knowledge, there develops a feeling of relative deprivation among one or a number of groups. As stated by Ernest Evans, "a previously dominant group may find its position threatened by another group that is better able to take advantage of the social and political changes taking place."[22]

The international community has been confronted with a series of difficult problems as a result of the end of colonialism and the process of modernization. One such problem has been the rise of numerous ethnic-nationalistic groups that have expressed their desire for statehood through the use of terrorist behavior. Groups such as the Basques, South Moluccans, and French Canadians have all expressed their desire for liberation through the use of terrorism.

The third cause of terrorism, closely associated with the ethnicity problem, is the decolonization of the Third World. The process of decolonization contributes to the current wave of international terrorism in two ways. First, the political borders of the vast majority of the decolonized nations were arbitrarily drawn with little concern for their ethnic complexion. The second result has been the rise of a political orientation in which the use of terrorism is viewed as a legitimate form of political behavior by a number of leaders of the now decolonized states. D. V. Segre and J. H. Alder, as presented by Ernest Evans, argued "that the reason why governments take a rather indulgent attitude toward terrorism is that it is frequently seen as a manifestation of the political and ideological struggles against imperialism and colonialism, creating an international climate conducive to terrorist activities."[23]

Another factor abetting the present wave of terrorism has been the writings by individuals such as Carlos Marighella, Mao Tse-tung and Ché Guevara. These individuals have greatly influenced the development of contemporary terrorism. However, the most influential author has been Frantz Fanon. Fanon's work *The Wretched of the Earth* is considered the most powerful and influential piece of literature written supporting the use of violence for political purposes. Ernest Evans has stated that "clearly Fanon has had a major impact on contemporary revolutionary ideology. His writing has increased the acceptability of the strategy of terrorism."[24]

Fanon's work is based on the belief that through violence the oppressed peoples of Algeria and other nations can rid themselves of their "inferiority complex and from [their] despair and inaction; it makes [the oppressed] fearless and restores self-respect."[25] Fanon views violence not only as a liberating force but also as a means to make "it possible for the masses to understand social truths and gives the key to them."[26] The writings of individuals like Fanon have acted as a guide and source of inspiration for those seeking to change their position through the use of violence. As stated by Robert Kupperman and Darrell Trent, "the writings of Mao, Guevara, Frantz Fanon, and Carlos Marighella illustrate strategy, foster a quasi-religious faith that history is on the side of the oppressed."[27]

Although the economic, political, social and psychological causes of terrorism outlined above represent an overview of the factors leading to terrorism, it is an incomplete picture. The post-World War II era has witnessed the greatest surge of technological developments in history, and these developments have made terrorism an international phenomenon. Brian M. Jenkins stated that developments such as "international travel and improved mass communications have provided terrorists with worldwide mobility and the availability of weapons and explosives; and new vulnerabilities in a society increasingly dependent on fragile technology have all participated in the spread of international terrorism."[28]

Terrorism is a form of low-intensity warfare. This type of conflict is waged over an extended period in which, as noted by Paul Wilkinson, the "terrorist observes no restraints or rules of war."[29] Whereas the terrorists play by their own rules, their opponents are constrained by moral and legal attitudes and institutional restraints.

Currently, the term *terrorism* has been used by government officials and the media as an all-encompassing label for the incidence of the numerous violent conflicts taking place around the world. The use of terrorism to describe the world's ills is a distortion of the phenomenon and, as stated by Walter Laqueur, illustrates "a basic failure to understand what terrorism is all about and what can be done about it."[30] A clearer classification of terrorism is, as outlined by Laqueur, "a specific weapon in the struggle for political power, employed either by groups of the extreme left or right but also quite frequently by national minorities."[31] He stated that "terrorism is violence, but not every act of violence is terrorism," nor is it . . . "identical with civil wars, wars of liberation or even guerrilla campaigns."[32]

The emplacement of concrete barriers around key U.S. government buildings in Washington, D.C., in 1984 after the destruction of the U.S. Marine barracks in Beirut in 1983, has nurtured the perception of international terrorists as powerful political actors able even to challenge the U.S. Marine Corps. Perceptions can be deceiving, and in this case they are. Terrorist groups are small and homogeneous organizations seeking unique political goals. Their potential power is restricted.

Terrorist groups are lightly armed, employing semi- and fully automatic weapons and explosives. Terrorists do not wear uniforms, in the classic sense, or any other form of identification that would separate them from innocent civilians. They move quickly and strike without warning. A terrorist group, as demonstrated by events in Lebanon, can strike anywhere, at any time and at anyone. A terrorist groups's ability to move quickly and strike without warning represents its only real weapon—that of surprise and fear. Its ability to instill fear and dictate the scope of its own actions, however, makes it possible to threaten the stability of the international community.

Terrorist groups are not guerrilla organizations. Terrorist groups are weak political actors. Unlike larger political actors, such as guerilla organizations, terrorist groups are confined to a limited range of actions. A terrorist group's range and scope of power is determined by the number and type of weapons it can deploy and by the amount of fear it instills.

GOALS

Terrorist groups have both strategic and tactical goals. On the strategic level, terrorism has produced a number of successes, most notably the formulation of the Irish Treaty of 1921 granting southern Ireland its independence and, arguably, the birth of Israel. However, there has been no strategic terrorist success during the past 25 years. Today's terrorists have been frustrated by an effective Israeli counterterrorist program, by highly trained military units such as the British Special Air Service (SAS), by the implementation of effective antiterrorist laws in nations such as West Germany and by a greater understanding of terrorism by many nations. However, although terrorism has proven unsuccessful strategically, on the tactical level "terrorism has proven generally successful."[33]

On the strategic level each terrorist group has its own unique goals, whether the development of the state or the destruction of a specific government. However, on the tactical level every terrorist group has more or less the same goals. There are a number of tactical goals of which publicity is by far the most important. A terrorist act is designed to produce media coverage. Through this coverage a terrorist group seeks to demonstrate to and inform the general public of its existence and create an atmosphere that promotes revolutionary behavior. As outlined by Robert Kupperman and Darrell Trent, "in order to be effective terrorists must inform and involve the general public."[34]

An act of terrorism is designed to influence four types of audiences. The first consists of the victims of the terrorist act. This audience may or may not also consist of members of the target audience. The victims of an act of terrorism are generally innocent individuals who happen to be in the wrong place at the wrong time. The victims of an act of terrorism, such as a hostage incident, represent an important psychological symbol to the terrorist(s). The terrorists' knowledge that they hold the lives of their victims in their hands represents a powerful psychological factor that satisfies their desire for power and self-esteem.

The second audience is the target audience, which consists of the population whose interests the group claims to be acting for or, as defined by Abraham Kaplan, "who is to be terrorized."[35] The target audience's response to a terrorist act is vital to the validity of the terrorist group's claim that it represents the desires and interests of its people. The current wave of terrorism plaguing Northern Ireland would not be possible without the target audience's passive or active support or its approval of the use of terrorist methods. On the other hand, one of the reasons for the failure of terrorist groups to operate effectively within the United States has been the failure of these groups to capture support from the target audience.

The next audience an act of terrorism is designed to influence is what Abraham Kaplan called the general audience, which "is usually referred to as 'public opinion', on a national or international scale."[36] Public opinion is a terrorist group's Harris or Gallup Poll. They are not seeking approval or disapproval for their actions but public awareness. If a wave of terrorism by a certain group fails to produce public awareness of the group and its goals, its campaign of terror can be labeled a failure. However, if a wave of incidents or one specific act produces an outpouring of harsh public statements by a government, public awareness is heightened, and the terrorist group's goal of recognition is realized. Public opinion is a gauge of a terrorist group's efficiency.

The final audience is the special audience. Kaplan outlined this audience as consisting "of potential rivals or allies of the terrorist."[37] An act of terrorism that fails is very damaging not only to the group's particular strategic and tactical goals but also to its reputation among rivals and allies. Not all setbacks are failures for a terrorist group. In the 1972 Munich incident, even though the majority of the Black September terrorists were killed by West German police and the rest were captured, they still achieved tangible results such as recognition and enhanced reputation. On the other hand, terrorist defeat and failure, such as that experienced during the successful Israeli Entebbe rescue operation, highlights the vulnerabilities of terrorism and seriously damages a terrorist group's reputation. The special audience represents an important source of moral, financial and equipment support. Access to these resources requires a demonstration impressive enough to illustrate the capacity to carry out a terror campaign.

A second tactical goal of a terrorist campaign is the disruption of a society's normal day-to-day routine through the use of intimidation and harassment of government officials. A terrorist campaign of coercion is designed to deny the target government both material and psychological resources. This form of terrorism has largely been associated with the decolonization process.

A third goal of a terrorist group, as pointed out by Ernest Evans, is "the polarization of a society by making the government more repressive."[38] Terrorist groups do not possess the capabilities to achieve their strategic goals. Instead, a revolutionary group seeks to polarize a society by exploiting its economic, political or ethnic problems or differences in the hope that the target government will implement policies that will further aggravate societal differences and alienate the general populace. The alienation of the general population will then, they hope, undermine the authority of the target government and strengthen the terrorist group's perception as a legitimate political actor representing the desires of the people.

The best example of a terrorist campaign designed to divide a society was the mid-1970s terror campaign of the Tupamaros in Uruguay. The Tupamaros, a Marxist group, sought to replace the democratic government with a Marxist regime through the use of terrorism, mainly the kidnapping of diplomats. In response to the Tupamaros' terror campaign, the Uruguayan government enacted emergency legislation empowering the military to take all necessary measures to stop the terrorism. Instead of leading to a Marxist regime, David Fromkin stated, "the terror of the Tupamaros bands led to a military dictatorship that brutally destroyed the Tupamaros, but did not lead to the predicted reaction by the masses in favor of revolutionary action."[39] Contrary to the Tupamaros' goals, a civilian president was inaugurated in February 1985 and democracy was restored.

Another tactical goal of a terrorist act or campaign is to influence or, as pointed out by Ernest Evans, "to aggravate relations between states so as to prevent a set of political events unfavorable to the terrorist group."[40] The use of a terrorist act to influence the relationship between two nations or to alter the pattern of regional developments can be illustrated best by the tragic destruction of the U.S. Marine Corps barracks in Beirut. The destruction of the barracks represents a successful attempt by a number of organizations, mainly the PLO, Syrian intelligence officials and members of the Shiite movement know as the Party of God, to influence events in Lebanon.[41] The possible goal(s) of these actors was to undermine American domestic support for the presence of the Marines in Lebanon. Facing increasing domestic opposition to the presence of the Marines in a hostile environment, the Reagan administration would be forced to withdraw the Marines, the centerpiece of the administration's policy toward Lebanon. The withdrawal of the Marines would then undermine both the multinational force and the authority of the Gemayel government. With the authority of the Gemayel government destroyed and the prestige of the United States greatly reduced, the door would then be open for those actors who were badly hurt by the Israeli invasion of Lebanon in 1982 to restore their influence in the area.

The bombing of the U.S. Marine barracks and the 1934 assassination of King Alexander represent terrorist acts that bridge the gap between revolutionary and state terrorism. State terrorism, as outlined above, is the threat or employment of extranormal forms of political violence, in varying degrees, by an established political system, against both external and internal opposition. The Syrian regime of Hatez al Assad had the most to gain with the withdrawal of the United States from Lebanon. Syria's aid to those involved in the bombing, while denied by the Syrian government, has been confirmed by different intelligence and press reports, such as the *Washington Post* article of February 1, 1984, entitled "Beirut Bombing: Mysterious Death Warriors Traced to Syria, Iran."[42] With the withdrawal of the United States and Israel, the Syrian government has been able to reestablish its influence in Lebanon.

A final tactical goal of a terrorist incident is the repatriation of terrorists and the raising of independent sources of funding, jointly achieved by kidnapping for ransom. The freeing of fellow terrorists is important to the survival of a terrorist group because if a terrorist knows or feels that attempts would be carried out to free him, the sense of brotherhood and unity that are key to the morale of the group will be reinforced. In addition, his loyalty to the group will be maintained and the ability of police officials to gain information is reduced. The small size of a contemporary terrorist group is another factor in the attempt to free fellow terrorists. The training of a terrorist is a complex process requiring time, equipment and money. The loss of just a few members of a group can cause major problems for a group, if not its destruction. The freeing of prisoners is important both for the group's morale and physical capabilities.

Even with the aid of certain nations, terrorist groups still need to secure funding from their own sources. The most effective means to both the freeing of prisoners and the securing of funds has been through the use of kidnapping of important individuals, normally businessmen and diplomats. There are countless examples of governments and businesses giving into terrorist demands.[43]

An objective interpretation of the goals and capabilities of international terrorists is important to any government if it hopes to deal effectively with the problem. In making the best possible decisions, a government must not underestimate or overestimate the strength of a specific group or that of international terrorism as a whole. The result of overestimating or underestimating the strength of the terrorist phenomenon is to distort its actual power. By overreacting to terrorism because of an overestimation of its actual capabilities, a government helps to fulfill the terrorist group's goals by possibly implementing policies that will alienate popular support away from itself and toward the terrorists. If a nation underestimates the strength of terrorism and chooses not to react to the terrorist threat, it, too, is promoting the goals of the terrorists. In not reacting to terrorist activity, a government faces the possibility that the terrorist group will develop an image of strength and viability in the eyes of the public. This will help a specific group and the terrorist phenomenon as a whole to grow in size and power. An accurate perception of terrorism is extremely important to a government if it is going to combat international terrorism effectively.

NEW ERA AND U.S. RESPONSE

As pointed out by J. Bowyer Bell and others, "there is no easily perceived beginning for this new era of terrorism."[44] The exact date or incident that has begun the era of contemporary international terrorism is not clear.

Until 1972, the international community was not overly concerned with terrorism. Before 1972, terrorist incidents rarely resulted in death or injury. Only an estimated 250 people were killed from 1968 to 1972 as a result of terrorism.[45] However, in 1972 the international community witnessed an increase in the occurrence of terrorism, with, as outlined by Brian M. Jenkins, "two particularly shocking incidents . . . , the Lod Airport Massacre in May and the Munich Incident in September, . . . appalling the world and provoking many governments including the United States, to undertake more serious measures to combat international terrorism."[46]

The U.S. response to international terrorism is based on a complex and broad array of programs designed to enhance the prevention of, deterrence of, response to and prediction of terrorist behavior. The United States defines *terrorism* as the "threat or use of violence for political purposes by individuals or groups, whether acting for, or in opposition to, established governmental authority, when such actions are intended to influence a target group wider than the immediate victim or victims."[47] In addition, it defines *international terrorism* as "terrorism conducted with the support of a foreign government or organization and/or directed against foreign nationals, institutions or governments."[48]

U.S. policy toward terrorism, in the words of Ambassador Robert B. Oakely, former Director of the Department of State's Office for Counter-terrorism and Emergency Planning and the department's designate Ambassador-at-Large for Counterterrorism until September 1986, "is direct." He stated that:

> We will make no concessions to terrorists. We pay no ransoms, nor do we permit releases of prisoners or agree to other acts which might encourage additional terrorism. We make no changes in U.S. policy because of terrorists' threats or acts. If U.S. personnel are taken hostage or endangered, we are prepared to consider a broad range of actions appropriate to the threat. We encourage other governments to take similar strong stands against terrorism. Finally, we are determined to act in a strong manner against terrorists without surrendering our basic freedoms or endangering our democratic principles.[49]

The heart of the U.S. anti- and counterterrorist efforts is a five-point comprehensive counterterrorism program, adopted in response to the bombings of the U.S. Embassy in Beirut and the Marines' barracks, consisting of: overt and covert intelligence operations designed to predict, deter and respond to terrorist incidents; diplomatic efforts designed to foster international cooperation, which is the key to dealing with terrorism in the long term; economic steps to increase the pressure on regimes aiding and/or abetting terrorism; legislative efforts designed to tighten U.S. criminal statutes so as to increase the penalty for involving Americans in a terrorist act; and military operations designed to punish those responsible for attacks against Americans. This program is based on the belief "that the primary legal, political, moral, and practical responsibility for dealing with terrorism abroad is that of foreign governments," and "if they do not have the political will or the ability to act against terrorism, the problem will get worse rather than better."[50]

The American antiterrorist policy and program is composed of a three-pronged approach made up of multilateral, bilateral and unilateral actions.[51] The *multilateral approach* includes the use of regional, multilateral, and international declarations, statements, agreements and treaties. The *bilateral approach* is comprised of bilateral treaties, mainly extradition treaties and memorandum of understanding between nations. The *unilateral approach* is based on self-help actions consisting of the implementation of economic sanctions against nations aiding and/or abetting international terrorism or the executing of military actions to prevent and/or deter possible terrorist actions or to rescue Americans being held hostage.

The U.S. three-pronged approach consists of antiterrorist and counterterrorist actions. It is important to state that antiterrorist actions are designed as defensive measures to prevent the occurrence of terrorism as opposed to counterterrorist measures, which are offensive in nature and are designed to respond to a terrorist act.[52] The following chapters examine the U.S. anti- and counterterrorist actions.

NOTES

1. Theodore A. Couloumbis and James H. Wolfe, *Introduction to International Relations: Power and Justice* (Englewood Cliffs, N.J.: Prentice-Hall, 1978), p. 344n.

2. Paul Wilkinson, "Three Questions on Terrorism," *Government and Opposition* 8 (Summer 1973): 298–299.

3. Richard Shultz, "Conceptualizing Political Terrorism: A Typology," *Journal of International Affairs* 32 (Spring–Summer 1978): 10.

4. Ibid.

5. Wilkinson, "Three Questions on Terrorism," p. 306.

6. U.S. Department of State, *Terrorism: Do Something, but What?* Department of State Bulletin (September 1979), p. 60.

7. Edward A. Lynch, "International Terrorism: The Search for a Policy," *Terrorism: An International Journal* 9, no. 1 (1987): 8.

8. U.S. Department of State, *Patterns of International Terrorism: 1982*, Office for Combatting Terrorism (September 1983), inside frontcover.

9. Robert A. Fearey, "Introduction to International Terrorism," in *International Terrorism in The Contemporary World*, ed. Marius H. Livingston, Lee Bruce Kress, and Marie G. Wanek (Westport, Conn.: Greenwood Press, 1978), p. 26.

10. Ibid.

11. *The Encyclopedia of Military History: From 3500 B.C. to the present*, 1977 rev. ed., "1914, June 28. Assassination of Archduke Franz Ferdinand."

12. Joseph Rothschild, *East Central Europe between the Two World Wars* (Seattle: University of Washington Press, 1979), p. 246.

13. Edward F. Mickolus, *Transnational Terrorism: A Chronology of Events, 1968–1979* (Westport, Conn.: Greenwood Press, 1980), pp. 321–324.

14. Ibid., p. 323.

15. Ibid., pp. 905–918, Christopher Dobson and Ronald Payne, *The Terrorists: Their Weapons, Leaders and Tactics* (New York: Facts on File, 1982), pp. 178–230; U.S. Department of State, *Terrorist Skyjackings* (Washington, D.C.: Office for Combatting Terrorism, July 1982), p. 9; idem, *International Terrorism: Hostage Seizures* (Washington, D.C.: Office for Combatting Terrorism, March 1983); idem, *U.S. Official Personnel Abroad, 1982–84*, Department of State Bulletin (April 1985), pp. 65–66; and idem, *International Terrorism*, Department of State Bulletin (August 1986), pp. 13–15.

16. Colonel James B. Motley, U.S. Army (Ret.), "Terrorist Warfare: A Reassessment," *Military Review* (June 1985): 46.

17. Ted Robert Gurr, *Why Men Rebel* (Princeton, N.J.: Princeton University Press, 1970), p. 24.

18. Ibid., p. 46.

19. Brian Michael Jenkins, "International Terrorism: Trends and Potentialities," *Journal of International Affairs* 32 (Spring–Summer 1978): 115.

20. Gurr, *Why Men Rebel*, p. 46.

21. Ibid.

22. Ernest Evans, *Calling a Truce to Terror: The American Response to International Terrorism* (Westport, Conn.: Greenwood Press, 1979), p. 15.

23. Ibid., p. 18.

24. Ibid., p. 17.

25. Dobson and Payne, *The Terrorists: Their Weapons, Leaders and Tactics*, p. 19.

26. Ibid.

27. Robert H. Kupperman and Darrell M. Trent, *Terrorism: Threat, Reality, Response* (Stanford, Calif.: Hoover Institution Press, 1979), p. 20.

28. Jenkins, "International Terrorism," p. 115.

29. Paul Wilkinson, "Terrorism: the international response," *The World Today* (January 1978): 6.

30. Walter Laqueur, "It's an Irritant, but Not a Mortal Danger," *The Washington Post*, 29 April 1984, p. B8.

31. Ibid.

32. Ibid.

33. Kupperman and Trent, *Terrorism*, p. 7.

34. Ibid., p. 41.

35. Abraham Kaplan, "The Psychodynamics of Terrorism," *Terrorism: An International Journal* 1, nos. 3 and 4 (1978): 239.

36. Ibid., p. 240.

37. Ibid.

38. Evans, *Calling a Truce to Terror*, p. 31.

39. David Fromkin, "The Strategy of Terrorism," *Foreign Affairs* 53 (July 1975): 690.

40. Evans, *Calling a Truce to Terror*, p. 32.

41. "Beirut Bombing: Mysterious Death Warriors Traced to Syria, Iran," *The Washington Post*, 1 February 1984, p. A1.

42. Ibid.

43. Mickolus, *Transnational Terrorism*, passim.

44. J. Bowyer Bell, "Trends on Terror: The Analysis of Political Violence, *World Politics* 24 (April 1977): 479.

45. Central Intelligence Agency, *International Terrorism in 1979* National Foreign Assessment Center, research paper (1980), p. iv.

46. Jenkins, "International Terrorism," p. 118.

47. U.S. Department of State, *Patterns of International Terrorism: 1982*, inside frontcover.

48. Ibid.

49. U.S. Department of State, *International Terrorism: Current Trends and the U.S. Response*, Bureau of Public Affairs' Circular no. 706 (Washington, D.C.: U.S. Department of State, Bureau of Public Affairs, Office of Communications, May 1985), p. 3.

50. U.S. Department of State, *International Terrorism*, Department of State Bulletin, p. 3.

51. Ibid.

52. Motley, "Terrorist Warfare," p. 48.

3

Coordination of the U.S. Antiterrorist Program

During the 1960s and early 1970s, the United States strongly supported the actions of the International Civil Aviation Organization and other international forums in dealing with specific acts of terrorism. Before 1972 the United States had no formal structure designed to deal with international terrorism. However, the Munich incident of September 1972 radically altered the U.S. attitude and response toward terrorism. Within hours after the Black September terrorists had killed nine hostages during a fire fight with West German police at Furstenfeldbruk Military Airport, the United States responded. The American response has had a profound and lasting impact on the government's ability to deal with terrorism.

THE NIXON/FORD ERA: 1972–1977

On September 6 and 7, 1972, Assistant Secretary of State Joseph Sisco and Deputy Under Secretary of State William Macomber were ordered by Secretary of State William Rogers to establish two committees to study the problem of international terrorism and to make recommendations on possible courses of action. On September 25, President Nixon, acting on the recommendations of the study committees, signed a Presidential Memorandum ordering Secretary Rogers to establish a cabinet committee and working group to combat terrorism.[1]

The Cabinet Committee to Combat Terrorism met for the first and only time on October 2, 1972. The meeting was attended by eight of the committee's ten members. The committee's full membership consisted of the Secretary of State (chairman), the Secretary of the Treasury, the Secretary of Defense, the Attorney General, the Secretary of Transportation, the U.S. Ambassador to the United Nations, the Director of the Central Intelligence Agency, the Director of the Federal Bureau of Investigation, the Assistant to the President for National Security Affairs and the Assistant to the President for Domestic Affairs.[2]

It was decided at the October 2 meeting that the committee would coordinate, evaluate and devise actions designed to enhance the U.S. ability to prevent and respond swiftly to international terrorism.[3] In addition, the committee was called on to make proposals on funding of antiterrorist programs and recommendations on methods to address weaknesses in the U.S. response to terrorism. Finally, it was to "report to the President, from time to time, on the status of American efforts in combatting terrorism."[4] The Secretary of State, as chairman, had the authority to adjust the membership of the committee and its working group as he saw fit. The committee on October 2 also approved the appointment of Ambassador Armin Meyer to the newly created posts of chairman of the committee's working group and as Special Assistant to the Secretary of State for Combatting Terrorism.[5]

The Cabinet Committee to Combat Terrorism was in existence from September 25, 1972, to the latter part of the summer of 1977. During those five years, the actual work of the committee was done by its working group, chaired by the Secretary of State's Special Assistant for Combatting Terrorism. Initially, the working group consisted of the same agencies as the Cabinet Committee. However, by 1974, 11 more agencies and departments were added to the Cabinet Committee and the working group: the Arms Control and Disarmament Agency, the Energy Research and Development Administration, the Federal Protective Service, the Immigration and Naturalization Service, the Law Enforcement Assistance Administration, the Washington, D.C. Metropolitan Police Department, the Nuclear Regulatory Commission, the National Security Agency, the Office of Management and Budget, the United States Information Agency and the Secret Service. With the addition of these agencies and departments, the antiterrorist bureaucracy then consisted of 21 organizational actors.[6]

The working group held meetings on a biweekly basis. During five years, the group held approximately 101 meetings.[7] For the working group's first two years of existence, the biweekly meetings were attended at times by more than 100 senior representatives of the Cabinet Committee.[8] Issues arising within the working group were handled on an ad hoc basis. The representatives of the chief departments involved (e.g., the Department of Transportation) would assign a specific agency or administrative unit to represent it (e.g., the Federal Aviation Administration [FAA]).[9]

By 1974, the quality of the working group's endeavors was being negatively affected by a number of factors. First, a number of agencies and departments within the working group were not exchanging needed information. Some members of the working group felt that information should be released only on a need-to-know basis. Second, the huge size of the working group itself was hindering coordination within the group. Finally, members within the group were losing interest in the working group itself.[10] In response to these problems, an executive committee was established during 1974, made up of only those organizations with jurisdictional duties in dealing with terrorism. These organizations consisted of the Departments of State, Defense, Justice, Treasury and Energy and the CIA, FAA, Joint Chiefs of Staff and National Security Council.[11]

During the summer of 1975, the American Society of International Law (ASIL) began work on a research project on international terrorism for the State Department.[12] The ASIL's research project, entitled the "Legal Aspects of International Terrorism," examined numerous aspects of the U.S. policy approach toward international terrorism, including the structure of the antiterrorist planning process and organization. The ASIL did not conclude its study until February 1977 and found that the Cabinet Committee and its working group were a good first step toward coordinating the U.S. policy response. However, the project's final draft report, as pointed out by Wayne A. Kerstetter, "recommended that somebody must be clearly assigned authority to respond to a crisis situation and that there be created a centralized data base on terrorist activities."[13]

On September 14, 1977, while appearing before the Senate's Subcommittee on Foreign Assistance, Brian M. Jenkins, a member of the ASIL's research project, outlined the major weaknesses of the Cabinet Committee and its working group. First, he stated that "while the chairmen of the working group were dedicated and capable, they were given no formal authority and lacked sufficient rank to impose their will on officials in other departments."[14] He also pointed out that bureaucratic politics were blocking the flow of information and thus harming the working group's coordination efforts. Next the State Department's rotation of personnel was cited as adversely affecting the quality of the working group's leadership. Jenkins stated that the different chairmen of the working group were being "compelled to learn about international terrorism on the job and they seldom remained long enough to apply the expertise they gained."[15]

Jenkins also pointed out that "terrorism is generally not regarded as an issue of major interest within the U.S. government."[16] This lack of interest was harming the American antiterrorist efforts and blocking needed reforms. Because of this lack of interest and the desire to protect bureaucratic territory, agencies dealing with terrorism were blocking corrective measures, such as the possible establishment of a single antiterrorist organization. These factors perpetuated the large number of actors taking part in the working group, the fact that "so many bureaucratic jurisdictions made governmental coordination difficult" and the conclusion that the "working group was primarily a bureaucratic coordinating body, not a command organization."[17]

CARTER ADMINISTRATION: 1977–1981

The election of President Carter triggered a major review and restructuring of the antiterrorist bureaucracy. Following President Carter's inauguration, a comprehensive review of the entire antiterrorist organization, entitled Presidential Review Memorandum on Terrorism No. 30, was executed. The review was designed "to assess U.S. abilities both to develop consistent policies for dealing with terrorism and to handle any specific terrorist incidents which emerge."[18]

By the summer of 1977 the Carter administration concluded its foreign policy review process. On June 2, 1977, the administration addressed international terrorism and the structural weaknesses of the Cabinet Committee to Combat Terrorism and approved the Presidential Review Memorandum on Terrorism.[19] The memorandum recognized the "need in the U.S. for a responsive, but extremely flexible, antiterrorism program at the federal level that would take into account both the contemporary nature of the terrorist threat and the wide range of federal resources that would have to be marshalled in any comprehensive antiterrorism program."[20] The memorandum also ordered the National Security Council to study the structural problems of the Cabinet Committee system and to make recommendations on possible courses of action.

By September 1977, by authority of a Presidential Directive (PD), the Cabinet Committee was dismantled and its role as the central coordinating body for the antiterrorist program transferred to the National Security Council's Special Coordination Committee (SCC). The SCC, consisting of the National Security Adviser (chairman), the Vice President, the Secretary of State, the Secretary of Defense, the Director of the Central Intelligence Agency and the Chairman of the Joint Chiefs of Staff (JCS), had three functions in the area of terrorism.[21] First, it was to supervise the senior–level interagency group to ensure coordination among the agencies dealing with terrorism.[22] The SCC was also empowered to resolve any jurisdictional problems that might surface during a terrorist situation.[23] During a crisis situation, it was to convene immediately. Finally, it had authority to ensure that all necessary decisions concerning terrorism were made at the highest levels of government.[24]

The dismantled Cabinet Committee's responsibilities were divided among two newly created organizations. The Organization for the Response to Terrorist Incidents took over the management of terrorist crisis situations and the Organization for Anti–Terrorism Planning, Coordination and Policy Formulation assumed the task of planning, coordinating and formulating governmental policy toward domestic and international terrorism. Both organizations were directly responsible to the SCC. (See charts 1 and 2.)

The Carter administration's September 1977 PD also reaffirmed the U.S. policy goals of deterring, preventing, responding to and predicting terrorism and embraced the concept of lead agency management of terrorist incidents.[25] By the time the Carter administration assumed office, the government had approximately 30 agencies assigned a role in combatting terrorism. There was no single agency, and there still is none, with jurisdictional authority to handle all terrorist incidents and policy–formulation functions. The lead agency concept was supported to clarify responsibilities and to minimize the impact of bureaucratic politics. It operates on the principle that if an incident falls within one agency's jurisdiction, that agency coordinates the U.S. response toward the incident. Working through the Organization for Response to Terrorist Incidents, only three agencies within the federal government have jurisdiction over terrorist incidents: the Department of State, the Justice Department/FBI and the Transportation Department/FAA.[26] Their exact areas of responsibilities are outlined later in this book.

The Organization for Anti–Terrorism Planning, Coordination, and Policy Formulation was, and still is, made up of multiple levels of organization, with the ex–Cabinet Committee's working group and executive committee constituting the upper two levels. Ambassador Anthony Quainton has stated that "their task was to ensure that there was timely, effective and detailed coordination among all agencies having jurisdiction or support responsibilities for combatting terrorism."[27] The executive committee is an Assistant Secretary–staffed organization "especially concerned with the response to major terrorism incidents and related issues, including periodic testing and evaluation of response capabilities."[28] A June 1979 report by the executive committee done for the Special Coordination Committee (SCC) also outlined the committee's duties as including "long–range antiterrorism program planning and analysis."[29] The Working Group on Terrorism did, and still does, meet "as necessary to carry out its assigned responsibilities, which included information exchange, resolution of jurisdiction issues, and the coordination of the general antiterrorism activities of the various agencies."[30]

As pointed out, by the mid–1970s about 30 organizations were involved in the government's response to terrorism. Because of the large number of officials taking part in the U.S. antiterrorism structure, the working group's ability to effectively integrate, draft and plan policy was undermined. In response, the Carter administration in August 1978 added five policy–review committees to the Organization for Anti–Terrorism Planning, Coordination and Policy Formulation. They were established, as pointed out by Ambassador Quainton, "in order to streamline the working group's operations and to maximize its effectiveness in policy coordination."[31] These committees, concerned with research and development, security policy, contingency planning and crisis management, public relations and international cooperation issues, represented the primary arenas of the working group's activities and were responsible for reviewing government capabilities to respond to a terrorist incident and make policy recommendations.[32]

The Carter administration was the first to feel the adverse consequences of international terrorism in terms of its political fortunes. As pointed out by Zbigniew Brzezinski, "largely because of the economy and the Iranian issue, the public lost confidence in Carter's leadership."[33] Carter supporters after the 1980

CHART 1

U.S. GOVERNMENT ORGANIZATION FOR ANTI–TERRORISM PLANNING, COORDINATION AND POLICY FORMULATION: CARTER ADMINISTRATION

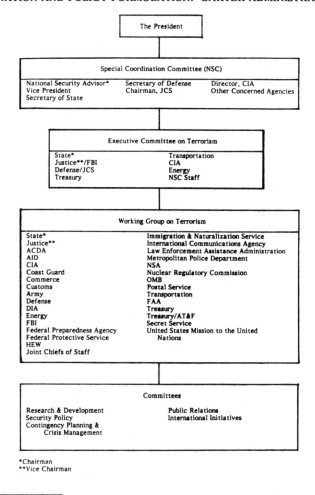

The President

Special Coordination Committee (NSC)

National Security Advisor*	Secretary of Defense	Director, CIA
Vice President	Chairman, JCS	Other Concerned Agencies
Secretary of State		

Executive Committee on Terrorism

State*	Transportation
Justice**/FBI	CIA
Defense/JCS	Energy
Treasury	NSC Staff

Working Group on Terrorism

State*	Immigration & Naturalization Service
Justice**	International Communications Agency
ACDA	Law Enforcement Assistance Administration
AID	Metropolitan Police Department
CIA	NSA
Coast Guard	Nuclear Regulatory Commission
Commerce	OMB
Customs	Postal Service
Army	Transportation
Defense	FAA
DIA	Treasury
Energy	Treasury/AT&F
FBI	Secret Service
Federal Preparedness Agency	United States Mission to the United
Federal Protective Service	Nations
HEW	
Joint Chiefs of Staff	

Committees

Research & Development	Public Relations
Security Policy	International Initiatives
Contingency Planning &	
Crisis Management	

*Chairman
**Vice Chairman

Source: U.S. Congress, House, Subcommittee on Civil and Constitutional Rights of the Committee on the Judiciary, *Federal Capabilities in Crisis Management and Terrorism*, 95th Cong., 2d sess., 16 August 1978, p. 60.

Note: NSC = National Security Council, JCS = Joint Chiefs of Staff, ACDA = Arms Control and Disarmament Agency, AID = Agency for International Development, DIA = Defense Intelligence Agency, NSA = National Security Agency, OMB = Office of Management and Budget, FAA = Federal Aviation Administration, AT&F = Bureau of Alcohol, Tobacco and Firearms.

CHART 2

U.S. GOVERNMENT ORGANIZATION FOR RESPONSE TO TERRORIST INCIDENTS: CARTER ADMINISTRATION

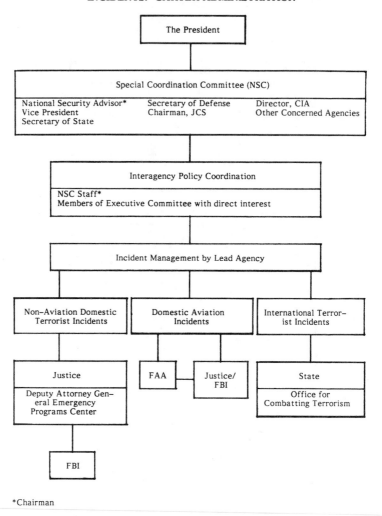

*Chairman

Source: U.S. Congress, House, Subcommittee on Civil and Constitutional rights of the Committee on the Judiciary, *Federal Capabilities in Crisis Management and Terrorism*, 95th Cong., 2d sess., 16 August 1978, p. 59.

Note: NSC = National Security Council, JCS = Joint Chiefs of Staff, FAA = Federal Aviation Administration.

presidential election, as outlined by Theodore White, have stated that the Carter administration's political future "probably died on the desert sands of Iran with the eight brave soldiers who gave their lives trying to free the American Hostages."[34]

President Carter's antiterrorist program and actions have been criticized by many. Former Under Secretary of State Richard T. Kennedy has stated that the Carter administration's antiterrorist program lacked activity and teeth.[35] James B. Motley, a senior research fellow with the National Defense University, echoing Brian Jenkins' statements of the late 1970s, has outlined the Carter administration's command structure as a "group merely providing a means of keeping in touch with one another, a useful but inadequate exercise. Real decisions were made in the individual departments and agencies."[36] However, it has been an acknowledged fact, as stated by Neil C. Livingstone, Director of Terrorism and Low-Level Warfare at the American Security Council, that "in the area of revamping the institutional machinery for dealing with terrorism, the Carter administration's record is a good one."[37]

THE REAGAN ADMINISTRATION: 1981–PRESENT

The election of Ronald Reagan resulted in no initial major structural or procedural changes in the American antiterrorist organization. The Reagan administration, finally, formally constituted its foreign policy structure in early 1982. The issue of terrorism was assigned to the Senior Interagency Group for Foreign Policy, chaired by the Secretary of State; it assumed the functions and responsibilities of the Special Coordination Committee. The Reagan administration retained the Organization for Anti-Terrorism Planning, Coordination and Policy Formulation and Organization for Response to Terrorist Incidents.

However, the Reagan administration, through National Security Decision Directive 30 (NSDD 30), has altered the structural complexion of the Organization for Anti-Terrorism Planning, Coordination and Policy Formation. The first change has been the renaming of the Executive Committee on Terrorism the Interdepartmental Group on Terrorism (IG/T). The IG/T's membership consists of the same departments and agencies, with the addition of the Office of the Vice President and the Drug Enforcement Administration, as its predecessor. The IG/T is seen as a "forum for the major departments and agencies involved in combatting terrorism to meet regularly and share ideas, draw conclusions, and make recommendations on policy and programs."[38]

The next change was the dismantling of the former policy review committees, because they were considered as ineffective.[39] Their functions were absorbed by the Advisory Group on Terrorism, which is the successor to the Working Group on Terrorism. However, in an effort to streamline procedures, four working groups have been established concerning technical support, exercises, training assistance and public diplomacy. The Technical Support Group is concerned with the research and development as it applies to counterterrorism procedures and acts as a "forum for the exchange of information and establishment of priorities." The Exercises Committee "focuses on crisis management exercises which involve interagency coordination as well as cooperation with other governments." The Training Assistance Group is designed as a forum "to ensure that there is no duplication of effort in U.S. Government anti and counterterrorism training programs in participating countries." Finally, the Public Diplomacy Group has been established in an "effort to coordinate, systematize, and improve ongoing efforts by several agencies to increase public understanding of the threat of terrorism and the importance of intensive efforts to resist the threat."[40] In addition, NSDD 30 reaffirmed the use of the lead agency concept for handling terrorist incidents.[41]

Although the Reagan administration has not radically altered either the government's antiterrorist policy or bureaucracy, it has redirected the focus of the American response to international terrorism. The U.S. response to terrorism from the early 1970s until the spring of 1984 was an approach based on a passive and reactive defense. However, on April 3, 1984, President Reagan signed NSDD 138. This directive represents a change in the American approach toward terrorism, in the words of former Deputy Assistant Secretary of Defense Noel C. Koch, "from the reactive mode to recognition that pro-active steps are needed."[42] The redirection of U.S. antiterrorist efforts represented by the signing of NSDD 138 illustrates such an important occurrence in the evolution of American policy and response, that a greater examination of both NSDD 138 and subsequent events is justified and is outlined later in this book.

AN ASSESSMENT OF U.S. COORDINATION AND POLICY EFFORTS

The U.S. response to terrorism has been severely criticized. Some have even stated that the United States does not even have an antiterrorist policy or program. Former Deputy Assistant Secretary of State Steve R. Pieczenik, who resigned in protest from the Carter administration over the handling of the Iranian hostage crisis, has stated in caustic terms that "the unpleasant reality is that we do not have a serious antiterrorist policy; it was left in a shambles in Tehran after being ignored for years anyway. Even if we did have a policy, moreover, we don't have the professionals or the organizations capable of carrying one out."[43]

The present antiterrorist command structure has been criticized and cited as being inadequate. However, as stated by James Motley, the present system has lessened to a degree "traditional interagency jurisdictional infighting and [is said] to have established a better working relationship among representatives of the Department of State and Justice, the FAA and the CIA."[44] In spite of these positive remarks, the caustic statement by Pieczenik is substantiated by recent events in the Middle East. In the span of 17 months, from the December 12, 1983, truck bombing of the American embassy in Kuwait City, Kuwait, to the September 20, 1984, van bombing of the U.S. Embassy annex in Beirut, four American installations were either destroyed or damaged by similar terrorist attacks, resulting in the death of 330 individuals in which 261 were Americans.[45]

During an interview with Cable News Network, Democratic presidential nominee Walter F. Mondale stated on October 18, 1984 that there is "growing evidence that no one was in charge of American foreign policy and security," and "'I don't recall any time in modern history where we've had one right after another of the identical threats, the identical acts, and steps not taken.'" He finally added a relevant question: "Who's in charge?"[46] Former Vice President Mondale's remarks must be seen in the light of a presidential campaign; yet, his remarks are still important. There were a number of intelligence reports warning of the possibility of another terrorist attack on American diplomatic institutions and personnel from the CIA and Israeli intelligence before the terrorist incident of September 20, 1984.[47] There were also warnings from the Defense Intelligence Agency and the Beirut Embassy Security Chief Alan Bigler of incomplete security arrangements at the Embassy Annex.[48] Yet American personnel were once again placed in a situation in which a successful terrorist attack, such as that against the U.S. Marines, was highly likely. Whether the fault of the policy that placed them there in the first place or through the American personnel's own lack of awareness or concern about the terrorist threat, Americans during 1983 and 1984 have died in a manner that raises questions concerning the U.S. antiterrorist organization and its coordination efforts and the quality of oversight by the Senior Interdepartmental Group on Terrorism in seeing that the proper information is distributed and the proper preventive measures are taken.

Further questions have been raised by current Congressional examinations into the U.S. antiterrorist organization and preparedness. On March 5, 1985, Ambassador Robert B. Oakley, then Director of the State Department's Office for Counter-terrorism and Emergency Planning, stated before the House's Subcommittee on Arms Control and International Operations "that before an antiterrorist plan can be implemented, his office must consult with other State Department agencies, the Defense Department, the Central Intelligence Agency, the National Security Agency and the White House."[49] Expressing concern and dismay over this arrangement, Representative Lawrence J. Smith (D–Fla.) asked the ambassador, "who in heaven's name is in charge here?" He continued by stating that "if the need for a preemptive or retaliatory strike should occur, it would take us a year to come up with a plan, and then we would be spitting into the wind."[50]

In addition, in response to the TWA 847 drama, Vice President Bush on July 11, 1985, while appearing before the National Press Club in Washington, D.C., announced the naming of Admiral James Hollaway, former Chief of Naval Operations and head of the review group that examined the failed Iranian rescue mission, as executive director of a task force to study the way the U.S. was dealing with terrorism. The task force under the leadership of Vice President Bush and made up of representatives from the FBI, CIA, Office of Management and Budget and the State, Defense and Transportation departments, in the words of the Vice President, "was to be certain that the U.S. was using every means at its disposal to combat this modern scourge."[51]

It is important that weaknesses in the U.S. response to terrorism are exposed and corrected. However, given the Reagan administration's past statements concerning swift and effective retribution and its criticism of the Carter administration's handling of the Iranian hostage crisis, one would expect that steps would have already been taken to correct problems in the U.S. response to terrorism; yet the administration's responses to recent terrorist incidents in the Middle East, including the raid on Libya and dealings with Iran, demonstrate a clear lack of understanding of terrorism and support the perception that the issue is being handled on an ad hoc basis. The growing menace of terrorism in the early 1980s and the disjointed and ad hoc approach by the Reagan administration arose in the mid-1980's Congressional concern that the government's response was dangerously lacking. This can best be illustrated by Representative Smith's comments, outlined earlier, and the conclusion drawn by three days of joint hearings by the Senate's Judiciary and Foreign Relations Committees, as presented by Edward A. Lynch of the National Forum Foundation, in the late spring of 1985, "that the U.S. has neither a comprehensive nor a realistic policy on terrorism. Current policy is fragmented and not fully developed. . . . No coherent strategy to either retaliate against terrorist attacks, or to prevent their occurrence, was apparent."[52] Unfortunately, the disclosure of the Reagan administration's arms–for–hostages dealings with Iran only reinforces this conclusion. The preliminary report of the Senate Select Committee on Intelligence on this affair, issued on January 29, 1987, demonstrated a policy making process in which key foreign policy actors, such as the State Department, were cut out. Junior officials of the National Security Staff, as far as evidence indicates, were able to formulate and implement an antiterrorist program completely outside the structure of the Interdepartmental Group on Terrorism, a State Department chaired organization. If the United States antiterrorism program is to be effective, all major departments and agencies responsible for its execution must be involved in the decision making process and those structures designed to formulate and oversee policy must be supported. The lack of support for a formal command and control structure leads to the destruction, not the construction, of an effective policy.[53] The next chapter outlines the roles of the key organizations in combatting terrorism and concludes by outlining a number of recommendations.

NOTES

1. U.S. Department of State, *President Nixon Establishes Cabinet Committee to Combat Terrorism*, Department of State Bulletin (October 23, 1972), pp. 475–480.
2. Ibid., p. 475.
3. Ibid.
4. Ibid., p. 476.
5. Ibid., p. 475–477.
6. U.S. Congress, Senate, Subcommittee to Investigate the Administration of the Internal Security Act and Other Security Laws of the Committee on the Judiciary, *Terroristic Activity: International Terrorism, Part 4*, 89th Cong., 1st sess., 14 May 1975, p. 220.
7. U.S. Department of State, *International Terrorism*, Department of State Bulletin (March 29, 1976), p. 396.
8. Laurence Gonzales, "The Targeting of America: A Special Report on Terrorism," *Playboy* (May 1983): 180.
9. U.S. Congress, House, Subcommittee on The Near East and South Asia of the Committee on Foreign Affairs, *International Terrorism*, 93rd Cong., 2d sess., 11 June 1974, p. 14.
10. Gonzales, "Targeting of America," p. 180.
11. Ibid.
12. Alona E. Evans and John F. Murphy, eds., *Legal Aspects of International Terrorism* (Lexington, Mass.: Lexington Books, 1978), pp. xv–xvi.
13. Wayne A. Kerstetter, "Terrorism and Intelligence," *Terrorism: An International Journal* 3, no. 1–2 (1979): 111.
14. U.S. Congress, Senate, Subcommittee on Foreign Assistance of the Committee on Foreign Relations, *International Terrorism*, 95th Cong., 1st sess., 14 September 1977, p. 67.
15. Ibid.
16. Ibid., p. 66.
17. Ibid., pp. 67–69.
18. U.S. National Security Council, *The United States Government Antiterrorism Program: An Unclassified Summary Report* (Washington, D.C.: Executive Committee on Terrorism of the Special Coordination Committee of the National Security Council June 1979), p. 2.
19. U.S. Congress, Senate, *International Terrorism* (14 September 1977), pp. 35–36.
20. U.S., National Security Council, *The United States Government Antiterrorism Program: An Unclassified Summary Report*, p. 2.
21. U.S. Congress, House, Subcommittee on Civil and Constitutional Rights of the Committee on the Judiciary, *Federal Capabilities in Crisis Management and Terrorism*, 95th Cong., 2d sess., 16 August 1978, p. 59.

22. U.S Congress, Senate, Committee on Governmental Affairs, *An Act to Combat International Terrorism: Hearings on S. 2236.*, 95th Cong., 2d sess., 23 January 1978, p. 8.

23. U.S. Congress, House, Subcommittee on Civil and Constitutional Rights of the Committee on the Judiciary, *Federal Capabilities in Crisis Management and Terrorism*, p. 56.

24. U.S. Congress, Senate, Committee on Governmental Affairs, *An Act to Combat International Terrorism: Hearings on S. 2236*, p. 8.

25. Gonzales, "Targeting of America," p. 180.

26. U.S. Congress, House, Subcommittee on Civil and Constitutional Rights of the Committee on the Judiciary, *Federal Capabilities in Crisis Management and Terrorism*, p. 56.

27. Ibid.

28. U.S. National Security Council, *The United States Government Antiterrorism Program: An Unclassified Summary Report*, p. 7.

29. Ibid.

30. Ibid., p. 8.

31. U.S. Congress, House, Subcommittee on Civil and Constitutional Rights of the Committee on the Judiciary, *Federal Capabilities in Crisis Management and Terrorism*, p. 57.

32. Ibid.

33. Zbigniew Brzezinski, *Power and Principle* (New York: Farrar, Straus and Giroux, 1983), p. 514.

34. Theodore H. White, *America in Search of Itself: The Making of the President, 1956–1980* (New York: Harper & Row, 1982), p. 21.

35. U.S. Congress, Senate, Committee on Foreign Relations, *International Terrorism: Hearings on S. 873*, 97th Cong., 1st sess., 10 June 1981, p. 47.

36. James B. Motley, *U.S. Strategy to Counter Domestic Political Terrorism* (Washington, D.C.: National Defense University Press, 1983), p. 55.

37. Neil C. Livingstone, *The War Against Terrorism* (Lexington, Mass.: Lexington Books, 1982), p. 248.

38. U.S Department of State, *International Terrorism: Current Trends and the U.S. Response*, Bureau of Public Affairs' Circular no. 706 (Washington, D.C.: U.S. Department of State, Bureau of Public Affairs, Office of Communications, May 1985), p. 3.

39. Interview, Kevin McConnell, International Relations Officer of the Department of State's Office for Combatting Terrorism, October 14, 1983.

40. U.S. Department of State, *International Terrorism*, Bureau of Public Affairs' Circular no. 706, pp. 3–4.

41. U.S. Department of State, *Combatting International Terrorism*, Department of State Bulletin (June 1985), p. 75.

42. "Preemptive Anti-Terrorist Raids Allowed," *The Washington Post*, 16 April 1984, p. A19.

43. "Terrorist Policy: It Could Scare You to Death," *The Washington Post*, 15 February 1981, p. C4.

44. Motley, *Strategy to Counter Domestic Political Terrorism*, p. 37.

45. "Issue of U.S. Embassy Security Stalks Another Administration," *The Washington Post*, 30 September 1984, p. A26.

46. "Eyeing Beirut Security Warnings, Mondale Asks 'Who's in Charge?'" *The Washington Post*, 19 October 1984, p. A4.

47. "U.S. Had Reliable Warnings Diplomats Were Bombing Target: Explosives Were Tracked to Lebanon," *The Washington Post*, 18 October 1984, p. A1.

48. "Embassy Staff Shift Defended: DIA Study Questions Facility's Security," *The Washington Post*, 23 September 1984, p. A29; "Security Chief Sought Delay in Annex Move," *The Washington Post*, 27 September 1984, p. A1.

49. "Antiterrorist Program Faulted," *The Washington Post*, 6 March 1985, p. A8.

50. Ibid.

51. "Admiral Leads Terrorism Unit," *New Haven Register*, 12 July 1985, p. 13.

52. Edward A. Lynch, "International Terrorism: The Search for a Policy," *Terrorism: An International Journal* 9, no. 1 (1987): 2.

53. U.S. Congress, Senate, Select Committee on Intelligence, *Report on Preliminary Inquiry: Iran–Contra Affair*, 100th Cong., 1st sess., January 29, 1987, pp. 1–65.

4

Agencies and Departments Comprising the Antiterrorist Bureaucracy

The U.S. antiterrorism policy is comprised of an array of programs and procedures. The foundation of these efforts is the federal departments and agencies with responsibilities. Currently, the United States has 30 agencies, departments and offices involved in executing its antiterrorist program. Outlined below are those federal organizations with a major direct or supportive role in combatting terrorism.

THE DEPARTMENT OF STATE

The most important federal agency combatting terrorism is the Department of State. The department, through National Security Decision Directive 30, is responsible for the implementation of American policy and programs dealing with terrorism occurring outside the United States.[1] The department's antiterrorism structure has evolved in accordance with the increasing occurrence of terrorism. As outlined by chart 3, the Office for Counter-terrorism and Emergency Planning, Office of Security and Office of the Under Secretary for Management represented the central components of the State Department's antiterrorism structure during the mid-1980s.

The Office for Counter-terrorism and Emergency Planning, created on February 9, 1984, represented the heart of the department's antiterrorism program.[2] Its primary functions were to "develop and recommend policies to deal with terrorism and to represent the Department of State in interdepartmental considerations on this subject" and to "conduct liaison with other governments on international terrorism policy." In addition, it was charged with receiving and reviewing "all intelligence materials from the intelligence agencies pertaining to terrorist threats and to take action as appropriate," which included working "with the Director of the Bureau of Intelligence and Research to ensure improved collection, coordination of assessments, and full utilization of intelligence community resources." Next, its responsibilities were to see that "terrorism alerts were provided on a timely basis to overseas posts, to approve all such alerts, and to monitor Embassy responses to such alerts; to [work] with other departmental units in setting physical security policies and practices relevant to terrorist threats, including coordination with other government agencies." Finally, the Office for Counter-terrorism and Emergency Planning was to ensure "the adequacy of Embassy emergency action plans."[3]

Before the creation of the Office for Counter-terrorism and Emergency

CHART 3

ORGANIZATION OF THE DEPARTMENT OF STATE FOR SECURITY AND COUNTERTERRORISM: MID-1980s

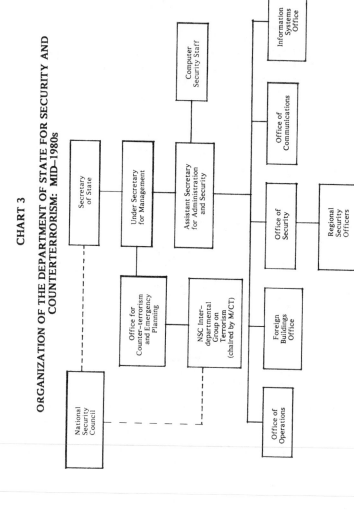

Source: U.S. Congress, House, Subcommittee on Arms Control, International Security and Science and on International Operations of the Committee on Foreign Affairs, *International Terrorism: 1985: Hearings on H.R. 2822,* 99th Cong., 2d sess., 5 March 1985, p. 48.

Planning, the department's antiterrorism duties were handled by the Special Assistant to the Secretary of State for Combatting Terrorism, from September 25, 1972, to October 1976, and then by the Office for Combatting Terrorism, from the fall of 1976 to early 1984. During the late 1970s, the Office for Combatting Terrorism was made up of six officials, not including the Director of the Office for Combatting Terrorism, handling both functional and geographic responsibilities, and three staff members. The officers' functional duties dealt with relations between their office and the press, Congress, the intelligence community, the Defense Department and the Department of Energy. Their geographic duties corresponded with the department's five regional desks: European Affairs, African Affairs, East Asia and Pacific Affairs, Inter-American Affairs and Near Eastern and South Asian Affairs.[4]

During November 1983, Congress approved legislation authorizing the Department of State to establish its long-sought-after U.S. Anti-Terrorism Assistance Program. The program is designed "to help friendly governments counter terrorism by training foreign delegations at U.S. facilities in anti-terrorist policy, crisis management, hostage and barricade negotiations, airport security measures, and bomb disposal methods."[5] The program's chief objective "is specifically directed toward enhancing the antiterrorist operating skills of relatively inexperienced governments and to expand cooperation among all concerned governments."[6] However, James Nathan, a Professor of Political Science at the University of Delaware, has pointed out another possible reason behind the formulation of this program. He pointed to a very disturbing international occurrence, which he labeled "New Feudalism."[7]

Because of the inability or lack of desire of many governments to protect the personnel and property of multinational corporations, these corporations have sought protection by hiring firms such as Payne International and Control Risks. These firms are not regulated and, depending on the firm, can engage in behavior ranging from negotiating with terrorists to the execution of paramilitary operations, as outlined by Ken Follett in his book *On Wings of Eagles*.[8] This situation raises serious questions concerning the effects on international stability. James Nathan stated:

> Those governments whose citizens are subject to terrorism in foreign countries are quite likely to view the counter-terrrorist firms as an effective means of protection that the host country has failed to provide. If this situation continues, the current international order may dissolve into a new medievalism in which private firms perform the security functions of the state, and citizens are left with little capacity to redress their grievances.[9]

Thus the goal of the Anti-Terrorism Assistance Program, in James Nathan's view, is to "reduce the need for private counter-terrorist firms and thus lessen the chance of abuses by these firms."[10] The Anti-Terrorism Assistance Program idea has gained acceptance by the U.S. Congress but not without some hesitancy, mainly from Democrats, who have "expressed concern that such a program could result in the United States helping authoritarian regimes clamp down on political dissidents rather than real terrorists."[11]

On February 4, 1984, the Director of the Office for Combatting Terrorism was assigned responsibility for administrating the Anti-Terrorism Assistance Program. Five days later, on February 9, 1984, the Under Secretary for Management increased the office's responsibilities by assigning it emergency planning functions.

These new responsibilities, in addition to those outlined above, expanded the number of duties of the Office for Combatting Terrorism beyond its capacities. In response, the Office for Combatting Terrorism was reconstituted and redesignated the Office for Counter-Terrorism and Emergency Planning on February 9, 1984. As of February 19, 1986, the Anti-Terrorism Assistance Program had trained more than 1,500 officials from 32 countries in antiterrorism methods and tactics. The program has been viewed by the State Department as "one of the most effective U.S. tools in strengthening the antiterrorism dialogue with other states and providing technical assistance in this field through training."[12] The program's success has eased Congressional concern over its possible abuse, and it increased support for it to the point of Congress adding $2.42 million to the program's fiscal 1986 budget.[13]

The Office for Counter-terrorism and Emergency Planning, like its predecessor, was headed by an ambassador with the title of director. However, the new office's staff consisted of 18 officials and staff members.[14] The office was divided into three sections. The first was the Counter-terrorism Policy Section, which was headed by a Senior Deputy Director and had assumed the policy functions of the office's predecessor. The next two sections were headed by Deputy Directors. One section deals with emergency planning and the other with the administration of counterterrorism programs, such as the Anti-Terrorism Assistance Program.[15]

The Office for Counter-terrorism and Emergency Planning had responsibility for the execution of the State Department's jurisdictional authority over international terrorist incidents involving American citizens and property. Working through the department's Operational Center, personnel from the office handled the American response to a terrorist incident by formulating a task force physically located in the center and headed by a representative of the counterterrorism office. The task force would remain on duty 24 hours a day until the crisis was resolved. The head of the task force dealt directly with the U.S. representative on the scene. This representative's main task was to remind the foreign government handling the incident of its international legal obligations to combat terrorism and protect foreign nationals. The American policy goal is to have the terrorist(s) punished either by the United States through the extradition of the terrorist(s) to the United States or by the foreign government using its domestic laws dealing with criminal behavior.[16]

The Director of the Office for Counter-terrorism and Emergency Planning was the chief U.S. antiterrorist official. The position of Director carried the rank of Ambassador with the administrative authority of an Assistant Secretary. The Director was the chairman of the Interdepartmental Group of Terrorism and through this position oversaw the U.S. response to both domestic and international terrorism.[17] The Director also headed the department's policy group on security policies and programs and contingency planning.[18]

The Director worked closely with the Office of Security. The Office of Security's primary function "was to provide protective security for the personnel and facilities of the agency and the Foreign Service in the United States and abroad, and for the protection of certain high level foreign dignitaries."[19] The office was headed by a Director with the rank of a Deputy Assistant Secretary. He was assisted by a Deputy Director and four Assistant Directors working in the U.S. Overseas, the Director was "assisted by associate directors in specific geographical regions."[20]

The Office of Security executed its domestic duties through its Domestic Operations Division, the Secretary's Detail, the Dignitary Protection Division and the Protective Liaison unit. The Domestic Operations Division "planned and administered security programs designed to protect the property and personnel of the Department of State."[21] The Secretary's Detail "was responsible for the protection of the Secretary of State anywhere in the world."[22] The Dignitary Protection Division "provided protection to foreign dignitaries (other than chiefs of state or heads of government) and their families while they are visiting the United States."[23] The Protective Liaison unit "maintained liaison with local, state and federal law enforcement and intelligence agencies, and foreign diplomatic and consular corps."[24]

The Office of Security fulfilled its overseas duties through the employment of a number of administrative and operational units. The Foreign Operations Division "developed and implemented security programs for the protection of personnel, property and classified and controlled information at U.S. Foreign Service posts."[25] The office's chief overseas officers were Regional Security Officers. A Regional Security Officer holds the administrative rank of an Assistant Director and is responsible for the formulation of contingency plans designed to cope with the different aspects of terrorism. These officers are also responsible for commanding, under the authority of the Ambassador, those Marine Security Detachments assigned to embassy duty. The Marine Security Detachments are the Office of Security's chief operational unit. The Marines, working with the Technical Services Division, provide protection of personnel, property and classified material. The Technical Services Division provides the Marines with the means of protecting the embassy from electronic penetration, surreptitious entry and terrorist attacks.[26]

During the late 1970s the Office of Security established a specialized Threat Analysis Group. The Threat Analysis Group is the backbone of the State Department's security programs. The group attempted to predict trends in terrorism in order "to enhance the Office of Security's ability to protect overseas personnel and posts and those dignitaries for which it has special responsibility."[27]

Since the November 4, 1979, takeover of the U.S. Embassy in Iran, the State Department has attempted to strengthen embassy security worldwide. The Reagan administration has placed a high priority on embassy security. However, events in the Middle East during the past few years, such as the car bombing of the U.S. Embassy in Beirut, have promoted criticism of administration's security efforts. On September 23, 1984, while appearing on "This Week with David Brinkley," Senator Joseph Biden (D-Del.), a member of the Senate's Foreign Relations Committee, pointed out that despite the State Department's spending 15 percent of its overall budget on security, security at many diplomatic posts was lacking. Senator Biden stated that Congress had given the State Department "half a billion dollars to do it: they've only done it to 10 embassies, only 10 are complete, and they've cut the list from 125 to 65. They have not done their job."[28]

In an attempt to improve security at more diplomatic posts, Congress in October 1984, passed legislation granting the State Department an emergency $110 million fund for fiscal year 1985. In a further move to improve oversight of the State Department's antiterrorism program, Secretary of State Shultz initiated on October 6, 1984, daily meetings involving himself, Under Secretary for Management Ronald I. Spiers, Assistant Secretary for Administration Robert E. Lamb, Director of Intelligence and Research David Fields and Director of the Office for Counter-terrorism and Emergency Planning Robert Oakley. When the Secretary is unable to attend, either Deputy Secretary of State Kenneth W. Dam or Under Secretary for Political Affairs Michael H. Armacost is to chair the daily briefings.[29] This development is a positive step, and it is hoped that this process is retained as a part of normal State Department routine. The benefits to intradepartmental coordination and cooperation are clear.

Before January 22, 1985, as illustrated by chart 4, a large number of organizational actors within and outside the State Department had a role in dealing with embassy security, and as illustrated by chart 5, a great deal of jurisdictional overlap and confusion existed concerning the State Department's handling of embassy security. In an attempt "to reflect a 'new reality' of growing terrorist violence," the Bureau of Administration, in which the Office of Security is housed, on January 22, 1985, was renamed the Bureau of Administration and Security.[30] Finally, in a further move "aimed at strengthening U.S. overseas diplomatic posts against terrorist attacks," the Congress on August 12, 1986 approved legislation authorizing the State Department to spend $2.4 billion from fiscal year 1986 to fiscal year 1990 on embassy security. The chief targets of this most recent security program were U.S. diplomatic installations in Cyprus, Jordan and Honduras. From 1984 to 1987, following the bombing of the U.S. Marine barracks in 1983 and the Beirut Embassy annex in 1984, the State Department has received over $2.5 billion for the improvement of security at U.S. diplomatic posts.[31]

Until the fall of 1985, both the Office for Counter-terrorism and Emergency Planning and the Office of Security reported to the Under Secretary for Management. The Office of the Under Secretary was responsible for seeing "that planning and policy, as reflected in the counterterrorism office, and the resources for the response to threats represented in the security office will both be under a single jurisdiction."[32] The State Department's senior-most official concerned with terrorism is the Deputy Secretary of State. He represents the department and chairs the Senior Interdepartmental Group on Terrorism.[33]

The need for current and accurate intelligence is very important to the success of the U.S. antiterrorist program. The Central Intelligence Agency, the Federal Bureau of Investigation and the Department of State are the United States' chief collection organizations on terrorism. The Bureau of Intelligence and Research is the State Department's chief intelligence arm. A more in-depth discussion of the U.S. intelligence community's role in dealing with terrorism is outlined in chapter 6. The Department of State also has three "attached" organizations with a role in combatting terrorism, the Arms Control and Disarmament Agency (ACDA), the United States Mission to the United Nations and the International Development Cooperation Agency (IDCA). ACDA is a supporting agency and has no direct role in dealing with terrorism; it is concerned with research and development issues, and provides information on counterterrorism technology, military equipment and the possible use of weapons of mass destruction by terrorist groups.[34] The IDCA is responsible "for coordinating governmental economic activities as they affect American relations with developing countries," and through the Agency for International Development (AID), it is also responsible for "administrating economic assistance programs overseas."[35] The AID is concerned with the possible termination of American funds to nations aiding and/or abetting terrorism.

The U.S. Mission to the United Nations is concerned with the coordination of United Nations efforts in dealing with terrorism. The United States has viewed the only long-term means of preventing and deterring terrorism as through international cooperation. A more comprehensive examination of the U.S. use of international cooperation and law in combatting terrorism is discussed in chapter 7.

In response to the growing threat posed by terrorism to U.S. diplomats and diplomatic posts, Secretary of State Shultz in the mid-1980s established an Advisory Panel on overseas security. Chaired by former Deputy Director of the Central Intelligence Agency Admiral Bobby Inman (Ret.), the Advisory Panel issued in June 1985 a report highly critical of the State Department's handling of diplomatic

CHART 4

OFFICES WITH EMBASSY–SECURITY ROLES IN WASHINGTON AND ABROAD

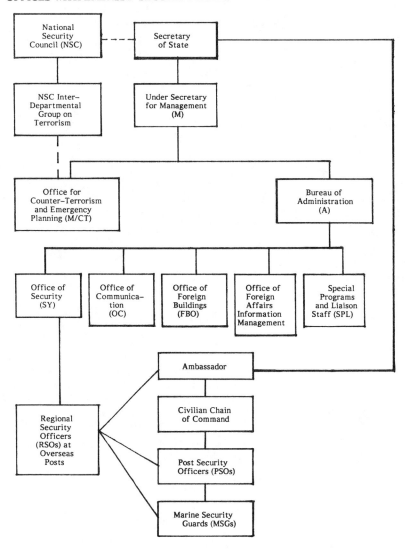

Source: House of Representatives' Subcommittee on Arms Control and International Operations.

CHART 5

OVERLAPPING RELATIONSHIPS AMONG STATE DEPARTMENT OFFICES WITH EMBASSY–SECURITY RESPONSIBILITIES

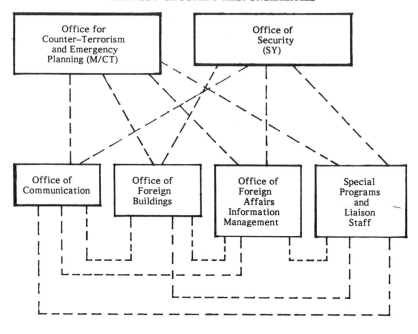

Source: House of Representatives' Subcommittee on Arms Control and International Operations.

security and terrorism. The Inman Report concluded that the State Department's approach to security and terrorism was suffering from chronic understaffing of the Office of Security, which was undermining training that was key to the office's success in implementing security programs; from insufficient funding to keep pace with the increasing clamor for material, services and professionals, which resulted in overlapping and confusing responsibility and a series of bureaucratic battles; and from an inadequate command structure, which was "not designed to meet the threats which have evolved."[36]

The Advisory Panel outlined a number of recommendations. The most significant were the proposed establishment of an Assistant Secretary of State for Diplomatic Security and a Diplomatic Security Service. The Assistant Secretary was pictured as the "principal officer of the new Diplomatic Security Service and should report to the Under Secretary for Management."[37] He was also seen by the Advisory Panel as replacing the Director of the Office for Counter-terrorism and Emergency Planning as the department's chief antiterrorist official, assuming the chairmanship of the Interdepartmental Group on Terrorism. In addition, the Office of the Assistant Secretary was seen as assuming the duties of the Office for Counter-terrorism and Emergency Planning.[38] The proposed Diplomatic Security Service as designed by the Advisory Panel was pictured as performing the functions of the Office of Security in addition to other duties. These duties would include security operations, engineering services, criminal investigations, protection of dignitaries and management services.[39]

Using the recommendations outlined by the Inman Report as a foundation, the State Department in the fall of 1985, as illustrated by chart 6, radically altered its counterterrorism structure. The Office for Counter-terrorism and Emergency Planning, the Office of Security and the Assistant Secretary for Administration and Security were replaced by the Office of the Ambassador-at-Large for Counterterrorism, the Director of Diplomatic Security Service and the Bureau of Diplomatic Security. This restructuring created a clearer division between security and counterterrorism functions. The Ambassador-at-Large for Counterterrorism, currently Ambassador L. Paul Bremer III, and his staff assumed the counterterrorism programs of the Office for Counter-terrorism and Emergency Planning. Now, however, the Ambassador reports directly to the Secretary of State instead of to the Under Secretary for Management. The Under Secretary lost his counterterrorism functions and assumed overall responsibility for the establishment of "policy and procedures governing the security of official personnel, facilities and information at home and overseas." The Bureau of Diplomatic Security, headed by an Assistant Secretary, assumed the functions of the Bureau for Administration and Security and the security duties of the former counterterrorism office. In addition, the Diplomatic Security Service replaced the Office of Security.[40] Only time can determine the effectiveness of these changes. However, continuity is the cornerstone to any successful policy; thus it is hoped that the State Department will not find it necessary in the near future to execute another major restructuring of its antiterrorism organizations. Such behavior only demonstrates and reinforces the image of confusion and inadequacy.

AMERICAN POLICIES AND TACTICS

One of most common targets of terrorism has been American diplomatic personnel and installations. From January 1968 through December 1981, the international community witnessed 2,856 terrorist incidents involving the world's

CHART 6

ORGANIZATION OF THE DEPARTMENT OF STATE FOR SECURITY AND COUNTERTERRORISM: FALL 1985–PRESENT

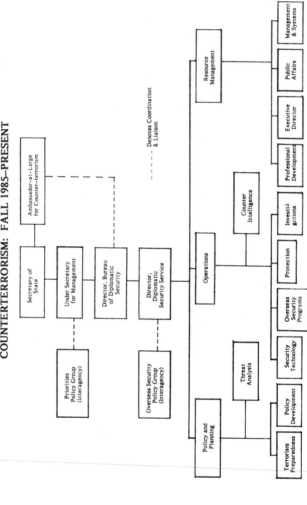

Source: U.S. Congress, House, Subcommittee on International Operations of the Committee on Foreign Affairs, *Aftermath of the Achille Lauro Incident: Hearings on H. Con. Res. 228,* 99th Cong., 1st sess., 7 November 1985, p. 36.

diplomatic community.[41] The American response to this threat has been one of periodic strengthening of its embassies and the development of a policy of non–concessions. This policy has been a constant feature of U.S. antiterrorist efforts since the mid–1970s, and as outlined by former Secretary of State Kissinger, the goals of this policy are "to save lives and . . . to avoid undue pressure on Ambassadors all over the world."[42]

The non–concession policy has been designed––in light of the March 1, 1973, Khartoum incident in which U.S. officials got involved in the unsuccessful attempt to free two American officials and one Belgium official being held hostage––to remove American officials and Ambassadors from the negotiation process to free hostages and to let the "terrorist know that the United States will not participate in the payment of ransom and in the negotiation for it."[43] Unfortunately, the creditably of the non–concessions policy has been severely damaged if not destroyed by the Reagan administration's willingness to trade arms to Iran for the release of American hostages. Administration officials, in light of this affair, look foolish and hypocritical in their support of the non–concessions policy and in the end only further demonstrate the Reagan administration's lack of a consistent and effective antiterrorism program.

One of the most controversial aspects of any nation's antiterrorist program is the use of self–help measures. Self–help measures can be divided into two categories. The first involves the use of force such as the execution of hostage rescue operations and special activities. The U.S. policy toward the use of these measures is examined later in this book. The second category of self–help measures consists of economic sanctions, international claims, diplomatic protests and quiet diplomacy.[44] Three of four of these measures are the direct responsibility of the State Department: international claims, diplomatic protests and quiet diplomacy.

International claims are designed to use the law of state responsibility in incidents in which there is evidence that a state failed "to prevent injuries caused by terrorism or failed to apprehend, punish or extradite terrorists."[45] Unfortunately, the ambiguous nature of the law of state responsibility and the likelihood that a state would not except responsibility for a terrorist act undermines the effectiveness of this measure. John Murphy, Professor of Law at the University of Kansas School of Law, however, stated that "the bringing of international claims serve a useful function in that they would focus attention on the illegal acts of the respondent state and raise the consciousness of the world community as to the legal principles involved and the respondent state's violation of them."[46]

The second self–help measure is diplomatic protest. Diplomatic protest, whether in response to a nation's failure to protect Americans or other nationals or in response to a nation's aiding and/or abetting terrorism, represents a worthy avenue of recourse. Diplomatic protest, first, states publicly the U.S. belief that terrorism and state behavior associated with it is illegitimate. Second, in the words of John Murphy, "the possible benefits of diplomatic protests . . . outweigh the possible costs."[47]

Because of the nature of international politics, the United States may choose not to use an international claim or diplomatic protest. As an alternative, the United States can engage in quiet diplomacy. Through the use of quiet diplomacy, the United States can still express its displeasure with a nation's behavior without the risks of both diplomatic protests and international claims. Quiet diplomacy also makes possible the formulation of agreements, such as the United States–Cuban memorandum of understanding concerning aircraft hijackings, which would not have been possible through more public forms of diplomacy.

One of the most debatable self–help measures is economic sanctions and export controls. The aim of the use of economic sanctions and export controls is to cut off military and economic support to those nations determined to have aided and/or abetted terrorists by the granting of safe havens and other assistance. The State Department views the use of economic sanctions and export controls against governments aiding and/or abetting terrorism as vital in its prevention and deterrance.[48] However, economic sanctions and export controls are not viewed by all sections of the U.S. government as vital weapons in combatting terrorism. The Treasury Department "does not view terrorism from an economic perspective."[49] The Treasury and State Departments have traditionally disagreed over the use of sanctions. The State Department, as outlined by Stephen D. Cohen, an Associate Professor in the School of International Service at American University, Washington, D.C., views "economic considerations as subordinate to the pursuit of a stable, secure, and prosperous international environment" that promotes "the general objectives of U.S. relations with other nations." The Treasury Department, on the other hand, views "the U.S. pursuit of a stable, growth–oriented, and fully employed domestic economy" as superseding foreign policy considerations."[50]

The State Department does not have exclusive power to impose either economic sanctions or export controls. It must work with the Departments of Commerce, Treasury, Defense and Transportation in imposing sanctions. Currently, there are an estimated 15 legislative acts granting the President the authority to impose economic sanctions on nations determined to have aided and/or abetted terrorism.[50] The United States has imposed sanctions on five nations for aiding and/or abetting terrorism: Libya, Iraq, the People's Democratic Republic of Yemen, Cuba and Nicaragua.[52] However, the unfortunate reality of economic sanctions, as demonstrated by the Reagan administration's imposing of sanctions on Libya, is that those nations aiding and/or abetting terrorism are not dependent on the United States for economic and military assistance. In addition, for sanctions to be effective, both time and international cooperation are needed. Yet neither are available in the required quantity. However, as outlined by former Assistant Secretary of State for Congressional Relations Douglas J. Bennett, Jr., "the threat of sanctions, whether automatic or not, is the significant deterrent. What is important is that foreign governments recognize the U.S. government will use its programs and authority when there is egregious behavior related to terrorism."[53]

The State Department is also involved in two programs designed to make travel by terrorists in and out of the United States extremely difficult. The Lookout and Forged Documents Identification Programs are designed to determine customs and immigration violations.[54] The Lookout System is a screening device in which all future visitors to the United States are checked for possible connections and association with known terrorist groups. The Lookout System grew out of the precautionary measures outlined by President Nixon on September 6, 1972, and in March 1973. On September 6, 1972, he ordered "visa procedures, immigration laws and customs precedures to be immediately tightened to screen more carefully potential terrorists seeking to enter the United States."[55] It is difficult to judge whether the system has been effective. However, during 1973, "a known leader of an international terrorist organization was denied entry into the United States because of tightened visa regulations."[56]

The Department of State is the United States' chief antiterrorist organization, employing and involved in a vast array of programs. Yet the department's approach to combatting terrorism, in the words of Ambassador Robert B. Oakley, "is suffering from internal confusion and we haven't been able to get our act together."[57] The Ambassador's remarks were made before the most recent structural changes, and it is hoped that a major member of the State Department's antiterrorist bureaucracy does not have reason to make similar comments in the future. However, there are still a number of weaknesses with the department's antiterrorism approach. The first is the position of Ambassador-at-Large for Counterterrorism. Terrorism is an important foreign policy issue, but it is no more a threat to the United States' national security than other issues such as nuclear proliferation. In addition, terrorists' chief goal is recognition; having a high-visibility counterterrorism position helps create the perception that their goals have been achieved. In an effort to avoid the establishment of an atmosphere sought by the terrorists and to place the terrorism issue in the proper context in relations to overall U.S. foreign policy, the position of Ambassador-at-Large for Counterterrorism should be joined with the Bureau of Politico-Military Affairs. In addition, all formal titles like that of Ambassador-at-Large for Counterterrorism should be eliminated.

The Bureau of Politico-Military Affairs is the State Department's primary organization dealing with political-military issues. It develops and coordinates guidance for issues such as nuclear proliferation and "maintains liaison with the Department of Defense and other agencies on political-military subjects."[58] The joining of the two organizations would, first, increase intradepartmental coordination and policy formulation between those departmental units dealing with terrorism and those dealing with foreign policy issues, such as nuclear proliferation and military assistance programs. Second, the unification of the two organizations would enhance interdepartmental coordination. The Bureau of Politico-Military Affairs' chief counterpart is the Department of Defense's Office of the Assistant Secretary of Defense for International Security Affairs (ISA). The Office of the Assistant Secretary for ISA is the Defense Department's chief antiterrorist organization, and thus enhanced coordination between these efforts would greatly improve the American response to terrorism. Unfortunately, the State Department's record of influencing political-military issues is poor. This record must be improved. Terrorism is a problem that must be dealt with within the context of the U.S. response to other political-military issues. The Department of State must be an active organizational actor in this area. The solution is what I. M. Destler, a member of the Brookings Institution's Foreign Policy Studies staff, calls an "alliance" between the Secretaries of Defense and State.[59] However, the "State Department needs a strong ISA."[60] The State Department's ISA should be the Bureau of Politico-Military Affairs, headed by a Deputy Under Secretary for Political-Military Affairs.[61] This organization would represent the State Department's chief antiterrorist unit. The Ambassador-at-Large for Counterterrorism would then direct the State Department's antiterrorist program from within this organization. The Bureau of Politico-Military Affairs should report directly to the Under Secretary for Political Affairs, for the Under Secretary represents the "highest position in the Department regularly occupied by a Foreign Service Officer (FSO). He assists in the conduct of foreign policy and overall direction of the Department, including coordination with other agencies."[62] The Under Secretary for Political Affairs should, one hopes, enhance interdepartmental coordination at the highest levels. The Under Secretary should assume the role as the department's chief senior representative to the Senior Interdepartmental Group on Terrorism, with the Ambassador-at-Large for Counterterrorism still representing the department on the Interdepartmental Group on Terrorism. The Under Secretary, generally being a FSO, should also limit the influence of domestic politics on the formulation and implementation of the department's antiterrorist program. In another move to place the issue of terrorism in proper order in relation to other foreign policy issues, the Under Secretary for Political Affairs should replace the Secretary of State as chairman of the daily meetings concerning terrorism involving the department's senior-most officials. The Secretary of State should separate himself completely from these meetings. Although the issue of terrorism is important, other issues, such as East–West relations, are vastly more important in terms of U.S. foreign policy and national security than terrorism and require the Secretary of State's fullest attention. Also, it is important not to inflate the importance of terrorism, and removing the Secretary of State from the daily meetings would be a positive step in this area.

A major problem the State Department and other agencies are faced with, in implementing the U.S. antiterrorist program, is the attitude of those officials carrying out policy. Ambassador Robert M. Sayre, former Director of the Office for Combatting Terrorism and its successor, has stated that "many U.S. diplomats have simply not understood the nature and magnitude of the terrorist threat against them. For example, General Dozier had been informed he was on a terrorist hit list, yet neither he nor his staff knew what to do about this and, as a consequence, did nothing."[63]

Events in the Middle East further reinforce Ambassador Sayre's remarks. Reports and charges of laxity concerning security arrangements at the U.S. Embassy Annex in Beirut have been cited as possible reasons for the successful terrorist attack of September 20, 1984.[64] In a related area, a 1982 General Accounting Office (GAO) report found that "inadequate planning, coordination and property management at the State Department was delaying essential physical improvements at U.S. embassies."[65] Although the GAO report cites bureaucratic battles between a number of organizations as the primary reason for the inadequacies in the State Department's security program, the attitude of department officials must also be considered. A major education and training effort is needed to correct this problem. The United States must improve the awareness of its officials by working either within the U.S. government or with the few major universities and colleges offering courses on terrorism.

A problem closely associated with the lack of awareness on the part of some government officials is the argument that terrorism is an issue best handled by specialists and not generalists. A major difficulty in the State Department's handling of terrorism—and that of other agencies'—is that key officials learn mainly on the job, but often before they can use the knowledge they have gained, they are transferred to another post. Witness the history of the tenures of the Directors of the Office for Combatting Terrorism. To address this problem, tours of duty should be stabilized "at three to four years, with no legal restrictions on extension."[66] The proposals outlined by the Inman Report and those mentioned earlier in this chapter represent compatible solutions to the State Department's problems in handling terrorism. It is important to correct the weaknesses in the department's antiterrorist posture because the Department of State represents the United States' commitment to combat terrorism. No matter how effective other agencies are in fulfilling their antiterrorist responsibilities, without an effective response from the Department of State, the American response to terrorism will be lacking.

THE DEPARTMENT OF JUSTICE/FEDERAL BUREAU OF INVESTIGATION

The Department of Justice, through the Federal Bureau of Investigation, has jurisdictional responsibility for all domestic terrorist incidents falling within federal jurisdiction.[67] The Office of the Associate Attorney General supervises the overall coordination of all agencies within the Justice Department dealing with terrorism.

Under the Associate Attorney General's authority are the Law Enforcement Assistance Administration, the Federal Bureau of Investigation, the Immigration and Naturalization Service, and the Drug Enforcement Administration. Presently, the Associate Attorney General is the deputy chairmen of the Interdepartmental Group on Terrorism.[68]

The Office of the Assistant Director of the Criminal Investigative Division supervises all antiterrorist programs conducted by the Federal Bureau of Investigation.[69] The Chief of the Domestic Security and Terrorism Section of the Criminal Investigative Division handles the day–to–day affairs of combatting terrorism.[70] The FBI's Special Operations and Research Staff (SOARS) is responsible for research and contingency planning.[71]

The FBI has a number of specific responsibilities in combatting terrorism. The FBI, through the use of Special Weapons and Tactics Squads (SWAT), is responsible for paramilitary operations inside the United States dealing with terrorism. The FBI has 59 SWAT teams consisting of five to seven agents, with one team attached to each field office. In response to "the growing threat of terrorism" and the perception that there was a "void in U.S. ability to handle a large scale terrorist situation," the FBI has formulated a 50–agent Hostage Rescue Team. The Hostage Rescue Team has been trained "to deal with a major scale terrorist incident with the objective of bringing out the victims alive."[72]

The FBI also has jurisdiction over the investigation of nuclear incidents involving terrorist behavior. The FBI is responsible for investigating all alleged or suspected criminal violations of the Atomic Energy Act. The mission of the FBI in a nuclear–threat incident is to take primary jurisdiction when question of the violation of federal law exists and, when appropriate, to coordinate the use of available resources in the interests of the public health and safety.[73] The FBI also has jurisdictional responsibility over hijackings in which the aircraft is not in a position to fly or is already airborne.[74]

All domestic terrorist crises falling under federal jurisdiction came under the authority of the Associate Attorney General. The Associate Attorney General is empowered to make all major policy decisions during a terrorist crisis. All major terrorist incidents within the United States are handled by the Emergency Operations Center located inside the FBI headquarters in Washington, D.C. The task force dealing with the crisis is currently headed by the FBI's Assistant Director of the Criminal Investigative Division. He is responsible for tactical moves, and the Associate Attorney General deals with policy matters.[75]

The chief tools available to the FBI in combatting terrorism are counterintelligence operations. The FBI has jurisdiction over domestic counterintelligence operations designed to be preventive and reactive in dealing with terrorism. All FBI counterintelligence operations must follow the Attorney General's foreign counterintelligence guidelines against "the foreign inspired terrorists or foreign based terrorists."[76]

Other agencies within the Department of Justice assigned an antiterrorist role are the Law Enforcement Assistance Administration (LEAA) and the Immigration and Naturalization Service. The LEAA's role in dealing with terrorism is a supportive one. Through its Office of Operational Support, the LEAA funds research projects "basically designed to increase U.S. understanding of the terrorist phenomena."[77] In general, the LEAA "assists state and local governments in all aspects of law enforcement and criminal justice."[78] It also performs four specific functions: development of public protection devices, public education, recruiting and training of law enforcement personnel, and organization and training of special units to combat crime.[79] The Immigration and Naturalization Service's primary role in the antiterrorist structure is its involvement in the Lookout System. The service's role consists of checking the names of individuals for terrorist connections "at the port of entry" into the United States.[80]

Finally, the Drug Enforcement Administration has been added to the growing list of agencies having an antiterrorism function due to the development of a new form of terrorist behavior known as narco–terrorism. Narco–terrorism involves the use by terrorist groups, such as the Shan United Army from Burma and the Columbia–placed M–19, and possibly some nations like Nicaragua, of what can best be described as drugs for guns. In an effort to raise large amounts of funds a number of terrorist groups and some nations have gotten involved in the trafficking of drugs. The United States has, through the Drug Enforcement Administration, only begun to develop a strategy for dealing with this latest form of terrorism.[81]

Unlike some of its allies, the United States has not been seriously affected at home by terrorism. Unlike international terrorist trends, U.S. domestic terrorists trends have dropped dramatically during the early and mid–1980s from 51 incidents in 1982 to only 7 in 1985 and 1 for the first half of 1986.[82] There are many reasons for this, one of which is the effectiveness of the Justice Department, mainly the FBI. The record of the FBI in dealing with terrorism is one of the few positive aspects of U.S. antiterrorist efforts.

THE DEPARTMENT OF TRANSPORTATION

The Department of Transportation has two administrative organizations concerned with terrorism. The department, through the Federal Aviation Administration (FAA), is responsible for the handling of hijackings and the oversight of civil aviation security programs.[83] The FAA's Office for Civil Aviation Security is responsible for the supervising of the security and safety regulations dealing with all aspects of civil aviation mandated by Title V of the International Security and Development Cooperation Act of 1985.[84] The FAA's security program consists of the use of random 100 percent baggage search, of x–ray equipment and metal detectors and of sky marshals on airline routes likely to be highjacked.

Recent interest in airport security was prompted by the June 1985 hijacking of TWA 847 in which U.S. Navy diver Robert Stethem was executed. Before the passage of the International Security and Development Cooperation Act of 1985, the FAA already had in place an extensive security program as mandated by the Air Transportation Security Act of 1974. The 1974 law requires all U.S. civilian air carriers to adhere to mandated security standards that cost annually approximately $75 million to $80 million to implement.[85] The rewards from the FAA's earlier security efforts have been the seizure of 19,000 weapons and the deterrence of perhaps 100 hijackings from 1974 through 1980.[86] Recent U.S. attempts at increasing civil aviation security are fundamentally concerned with the security programs of other nations. Perhaps the greatest success the United States has had in combatting terrorism has been the almost total elimination of hijackings of aircraft using U.S. facilities and airspace.

Working with the International Air Transportation Association, the FAA surveys the security programs of other nations to see that the minimum standards for airport safety and security set down by the International Civil Aviation Organization are being adhered to. The Secretary of Transportation, by virtue of Section 1115(b) of the Antihijacking Act of 1974 and the International Security and Development Cooperation Act of 1985, has the authority to suspend American civil aviation traffic with any nation that does not maintain the minimum airport-security measures mandated by the Hague Convention of 1970. In addition, the Antihijacking Act of 1974 empowers the Secretary of Transportation to suspend American civil aviation traffic with any nation that aids and/or abets terrorism.[87] However, in both cases, the Secretary must have the approval of the Secretary of State before such actions can be taken.

The FAA's main responsibility is the handling of crisis situations involving U.S. civilian aircraft. The FAA's mandated authority covers the "hijackings of aircraft in flight or on the ground with its doors closed."[88] Because hijacking incidents invade the jurisdictional realms of other federal departments, the FAA has formulated memoranda of understandings with the FBI and with the State and Defense Departments. These memoranda outline agency responsibilities dealing with domestic and international hijackings and hijackings involving U.S. military bases.[89]

The second department unit dealing with terrorism is the United States Coast Guard (USCG). The USCG and the U.S. Navy, in the wake of the Achille Lauro incident and the ever-present danger to offshore oil rigs, have begun to address this aspect of terrorism. The growing dependence by the United States and its allies on offshore oil has raised concerns over the possibility of terrorist attacks on offshore oil platforms.[90] The USCG is responsible for the enforcement of maritime law, the protection of commercial vessels and port safety and security. The USCG's responsibilities extend over all U.S. territorial waters. The nature of the USCG's duties creates the possibility of a jurisdictional conflict with the FBI when a terrorist incident occurs within the borders of a U.S. port facility. To avoid a jurisdictional conflict, the USCG and the FBI have formulated a memorandum of understanding that calls for "close coordination and cooperation and the pooling of resources."[91] Currently, the USCG has placed greater emphasis on issues other than terrorism. Narcotics control and the flow of refugees from the Caribbean Basin nations are presently the USCG's major concerns.

NUCLEAR POWER AND TERRORISM

The most terrifying aspect of terrorism is the possible use by a terrorist group of a weapon of mass destruction, mainly a nuclear weapon. Within the U.S. government there are three agencies assigned to deal with the technical aspects involved in this threat. The Department of Defense has jurisdiction over technical matters involving nuclear weapons. The Nuclear Regulatory Commission (NRC) has authority over technical problems involved with a terrorist incident in which nuclear material is used for civilian purposes. Third, the Department of Energy is responsible for incidents involving nuclear material used for military purposes but not in the form of a weapon.[92] As mandated by the Atomic Energy Act of 1954 and the Energy Reorganization Act of 1974, the NRC is responsible for the licensing and regulation of "atomic energy power plants, the possession, transfer and use of special nuclear materials, and import and exports of nuclear facilities and materials."[93] Its licensing authority empowers it to deny export licenses for nuclear materials going to nations aiding and/or abetting terrorism.[94]

Through its Office of Nuclear Material Safety and Safeguards, the NRC supervises the maintenance of protection procedures "against threats, thefts and sabotage of licensed facilities and material."[95] This office also works alongside the International Atomic Energy Agency in checking the security programs of foreign nuclear facilities handling U.S. licensed nuclear material.

The Department of Energy

The Department of Energy (DOE), represented by its Office of the Assistant Secretary for Defense Programs, is involved in the planning for and response to the use of a nuclear devise by a terrorist group. The Assistant Secretary has three responsibilities. First, he is responsible for the "overall planning and preparedness for emergencies involving nuclear weapons or components in the Department of Energy's custody, or significant quantities of governmental–owned special nuclear material in transit." The Assistant Secretary is also in charge of "the overall planning and preparedness for Department of Energy's response for terrorist threats of acts, natural disasters and national emergencies." Finally, the Assistant Secretary is responsible for maintaining a liaison between his department and other preparedness agencies.[96]

The chief asset of the DOE in dealing with a nuclear terrorist incident is its Nuclear Emergency Search Team (NEST). The NEST provides technical assistance to the FBI during a nuclear incident. Operational control of the NEST is exercised by the department's Nevada Operations Office, which is responsible "for the planning and execution of all departmental operations designed for the search and identification of any ionizing radiation producing materials which may have been lost or stolen, or may be associated with bomb threats and/or radiation dispersal threats without geographical limitations."[97]

The Department of Energy, through its Transportation Safeguards Division, is also responsible for the transport of "inactivated atomic and hydrogen bombs, nuclear cannon shells, missile warheads, atomic land mines, weapons–grade uranium and plutonium, and classified but non–nuclear trigger parts for hydrogen bombs." Currently, the Transportation Safeguards Division has 30 heavily armored trailers, manned by a heavily armed crew of two. This program carries the department's highest security classification.[98]

THE FEDERAL EMERGENCY MANAGEMENT AGENCY

To enhance the coordination of crisis–management and contingency–planning efforts of the vast number of government agencies dealing with terrorism in particular and crisis management in general, President Carter issued executive order 12148 on July 20, 1979. Executive order 12148 established the Federal Emergency Management Agency (FEMA). FEMA replaced the General Services Administration and other agencies involved in the area of disaster–preparedness planning. In dealing with terrorist incidents, FEMA is responsible "for the coordination of preparedness and planning to reduce the consequences of a major terrorist incident."[99]

The Federal Emergency Management Agency functions as a central coordination organization. Its responsibilities do not replace the preparedness functions of other agencies dealing with terrorism and do not supercede the jurisdiction of those agencies dealing directly with terrorism. Robert Kupperman, Executive Director of Georgetown University's Center for Strategic and International Studies, and Darrell Trent, Senior Research Fellow at the Hoover Institution at Stanford University, cite this as a weakness that demonstrates FEMA's lack of clout. They state that "a possible shortcoming of the new Federal Emergency Management Agency is that the new agency has the same status as all the other agencies."[100] However, FEMA does represent an improvement in American crisis management and contingency planning.

THE DEPARTMENT OF COMMERCE

From 1968 through 1981, 3,206 terrorist attacks were carried out against American citizens and property.[101] Until 1980, American business executives and facilities suffered the most at the hands of terrorists. Approximately 953 terrorist attacks from 1968 to 1981 involved American business facilities and executives.[102] Within the U.S. government, the Department of Commerce, in cooperation with the State Department, "advises private corporations and their employees how to protect themselves and their property against terrorist attacks."[103] The Commerce and State Departments have attempted to convince U.S. corporations to follow the American policy of not paying ransom to terrorists in the hope of reducing the pressure on U.S. business interests overseas. However, it is not illegal to pay ransom, and U.S. corporations have at times chosen to fulfill terrorist demands. For this reason, and others, U.S. business facilities and executives stationed overseas have for the past two decades been a prime target of terrorists. Terrorists have asked for and received ransom payments, sometimes in the amount of millions of dollars. An example is the case of John R. Thompson, President and General Manager of Firestone Tire and Rubber Company's subsidiary in Buenos Aires. Thompson was kidnapped on June 18, 1973, and only after the payment of a $3 million ransom was he released on July 6, 1973.[104] The Commerce Department can only advise U.S. corporations on how to deal with terrorism.

The Department of Commerce's functions in dealing with terrorism are both supportive and direct. The department, working with other agencies through the Office of the Deputy Assistant Secretary for Industry and Trade and the Office of Export Administration, regulates export licenses for all exportable products. The Deputy Assistant Secretary and the Office of Export Administration have the authority to deny licenses for any product going to a government that the Secretary of State has determined aids and/or abets terrorism.[105] As already stated, the use of export controls and economic sanctions are viewed by components of the U.S. government as vital in deterring and preventing terrorism. The goal being the elimination of safe havens for terrorists. By pressuring nations with economic sanctions the United States is seeking to leave no place for terrorists to hide from prosecution.

The Commerce Department supportive role is executed by the National Technical Information Service. The service provides scientific, technical and engineering information concerned with addressing specific problems in dealing with terrorism. The service is also involved with the screening of governmental technical information that can be of assistance to a terrorist group.[106]

THE DEPARTMENT OF THE TREASURY

The Treasury Department deals with terrorism through a law-enforcement perspective. The department has both a law-enforcement function and the authority to use economic levers in combatting terrorism. All of the Treasury Department's antiterrorist law-enforcement activity is coordinated by the Assistant Secretary for Enforcement and Operations.[107]

Under the Assistant Secretary's jurisdiction are the Secret Service, the Customs Service and the Bureau of Alcohol, Tobacco and Firearms. The Customs Service is the central component of the Lookout System. The service physically examines the baggage and packages of individuals entering the United States and searches for possible terrorists and their equipment. The Secret Service, through its Office of the Executive Protective Services, is responsible for the protection of visiting dignitaries of the rank of Chief of State or Prime Minister and others that the President might designate. The Secret Service also provides physical security for foreign diplomatic installations. However, the Secret Service's main task is the protection of the President and the Vice President and any other federal officials the President orders protected. The Bureau of Alcohol, Tobacco and Firearms represents the Treasury Department in terrorist incidents involving the use of explosives. The Treasury Department has formulated a memorandum of understanding with the FBI addressing this issue. During an investigation of an incident involving explosives, the FBI acts in the role of supervisor, and the Bureau of Alcohol, Tobacco and Firearms handles technical matters.[108]

The Treasury Department also supervises U.S. participation in the International Monetary Fund. By virtue of Public Law 95–118, section 701 (a) (2), the Secretary of the Treasury has the authority over the American representatives to the International Monetary Fund, the International Bank for Reconstruction and Development, the International Development Association, the International Finance Corporation, the Inter–American Development Bank, the African Development Fund and the Asian Development Bank to deny U.S. aid to any nation that "provides refuge to individuals committing acts of international terrorism."[109]

RECOMMENDATIONS

To develop an effective U.S. response to terrorism, a series of important corrective steps are needed. However, an awareness of some important characteristics of the U.S. governmental structure and process are critical to the success or failure of any attempt to improve the American response to terrorism. The first characteristic is the influence of bureaucratic politics on the policy–formulation process. As witnessed by the behavior of the former Cabinet Committee's working group in the 1970s, bureaucratic politics have had a major impact. Any attempt to improve the American response to terrorism must work within the confines set down by the nature of bureaucratic politics.

One of the most–cited solutions to this problem has been either the creation of a new organization with jurisdiction over all aspects of the American response or the placing in an existing agency over all jurisdiction. However, this solution fails to take into account the nature of terrorism and the influence of bureaucratic politics. Terrorism is a complex phenomenon requiring a comprehensive response. No agency within the U.S. government possesses the vast array of capabilities needed to combat terrorism effectively. It would be difficult, if not impossible, to create a single department with the needed jurisdiction to control the U.S. response to terrorism and other problems and priorities the U.S. government has to deal with and would lead to even greater policy and process problems.

The next characteristic of the governmental process is the influence of domestic politics. It has been stated that the President must avoid personal involvement in the U.S. response to terrorism.[110] This is politically unrealistic. However, the terrorism issue must not be politicized and must remain a bipartisan issue. It would be unrealistic and unwise for an American President to divorce himself from the formulation of the U.S. antiterrorist program. A President is ultimately responsible, or should be, for all decisions made by his administration; he alone has the authority and influence, if used, to ensure that policy decisions are carried out. For the U.S. response to terrorism to be effective, it must involve the entire government.

The Carter administration's Iran crisis and that of the Reagan administration illustrate how important it is that the President's role in the formulation and implementation of U.S. antiterrorism policy be clearly defined. In both cases the Presidents developed such a deep personal concern for the welfare of the American hostages that it led their administrations becoming overly occupied with the issue. Presidents Carter and Reagan, however, handled their respective incidents in diametrically different ways, as dictated by their individual management styles. President Carter became so involved in the execution of his administration's efforts to release the American hostages that he altered his 1980 reelection campaign schedule so as to remain close to the White House and the management of the crisis. He even became involved not only in strategic questions but tactical matters as well. President Reagan, on the other hand, while consistently expressing concern over the welfare of the hostages, divorced himself from the formulation and execution of his administration's efforts to release them. He did so to such an extent that he was unable, once the Iran arms–for–hostages affair was exposed, to explain his administration's behavior. President Reagan's inability to adequately explain his administration's behavior led to accusations of Presidential incompetence. It is felt that if the President did not know what officials in his administration were doing, he should have.

The President has a number of very important duties in the formulation and execution of United States antiterrorism policy. The first is seeing that his administration and himself have placed the terrorism issue in the proper order of importance in relation to other foreign policy considerations. The terrorism issue stirs powerful personal and nationalistic feelings. It is only natural to want to help the victims of terrorism. However, it is important to remember that the terrorists' chief tactical goals are publicity and recognition. An administration works against its goals of deterring, preventing and suppressing terrorism and helping its victims when it places the issue above other more important foreign policy considerations, such as arms control, because it is granting the recognition the terrorists are seeking. A President, no matter how he feels about the issue of terrorism, must maintain an objective outlook on what foreign policy issues his administration must deal with first in order to promote and protect U.S. interests. This is associated with the President's second antiterrorism function. A President, while he may express concern for the welfare of a few Americans being held hostage, is responsible for the protection of United States' interests and the welfare of all Americans. One of the most unfortunate aspects of the Iran arms–for–hostages affair is that President Reagan allowed his personal concern for the welfare of the hostages being held in Lebanon to influence his judgment to the point that he supported a policy that in the end will increase the occurrence of terrorism instead of decreasing it and thus place a greater number of Americans at risk. It is fine for Ronald Reagan to demonstrate compassion for the welfare of the hostages but President Reagan must temper his personal concerns with his responsibilities as President of the United States. Finally, the President sets the tone and direction of his administration's policies, whether it be dealing with terrorism or any other issue. One of the most important aspects of any policy toward terrorism is continuity and consistency. Perhaps the most shocking and disappointing aspect of the Iran arms–for–hostages affair is that President Reagan since January 1981 had stated that the United States would not deal with terrorists, but in the end he did exactly that. No other aspect of the whole affair has done more to destroy the creditability of the President's and his administration's antiterrorism policy than his violation of his own standards. No other government official has a more vital or complex role to play in the formulation and execution of United States antiterrorism policy then the President. His ability and success in fulfilling this role is a major factor in determining the success or failure of his administration's response to international terrorism.

The first major step in constructing an effective antiterrorist program is a major review of U.S. foreign and national security objectives and policy. William J. Taylor, Jr., Deputy Chief Operating Officer at the Georgetown University for Strategic and International Studies, and Steve A. Maaranen, staff member of the Office of Planning and Analysis, Los Alamos National Laboratory, have stated that "clearly, our planning needs to proceed and be governed by strategic guidance, and that guidance must be based on careful thinking about the environment of the 1980s. That environment will abound with conflicts requiring responses quite unconventional for U.S. planners."[111]

In response to the unconventional threats of the 1980s and 1990s, U.S. policy "should be supported by strategies which *prevent* indigenous or regional conditions which might prove inimical to our interests or prompt external involvement, *deter* external involvement if prevention fails and *compel* those who would directly threaten our interests to desist if deterrence fails."[112]

The next major step is the restructuring of the present command structure of the antiterrorist bureaucracy. The first modification, as cited by James Motley, a senior research fellow with the National Defense University, should be to "retitle the current U.S. antiterrorist program in order to portray better the priority assigned to this aspect of internal and national security and the actual roles of departments and agencies."[113] Motley pointed out a valid issue with his questioning of the desirability of formally naming the U.S. antiterrorist program. The major tactical goals of a terrorist group are publicity and recognition. "Then one wonders if giving the program a formal title may actually help terrorism inflate its own importance."[114] Not only is retitling the formal command structure recommended but also eliminating titles like that of the Department of State's Ambassador-at-Large for Counterterrorism, if not the actual elimination of this type of office. Each major department involved in combatting terrorism should establish an integrated organization encompassing all of those officials and resources involved and used in that department's antiterrorist efforts. Each departmental organization should be a policy formulation body and command authority with the power to control all aspects of its program and should be administered by an official with an administrative rank no less than that of an Under Secretary. This action would help coordinate and implement the department's own responsibilities and would cut down on the number of actors involved in the interdepartmental area.

The next modification should be the establishment of an office within the Executive Office of the President, which should "serve as the focal point for the oversight of the U.S. antiterrorist program."[115] Brian M. Jenkins of the Rand Corporation has presented the executive staff or office as:

> a permanent body with a White House perspective; such a staff could monitor and coordinate activities of the line agency and departments; identity needed capabilities; identify special resources that might be mobilized if an international incident occurs; pull together current intelligence and ongoing analysis and research efforts; identify

terrorist incidents; develop scenarios and formulate plans. It would see to it that the necessary resources and capabilities are there when they are needed. In an actual crisis, it could function as a small battle staff for decision-makers.[116]

This staff should be a component of the National Security Council and headed by an official with the administrative authority of that of a Deputy Assistant for National Security Affairs. This official should be a specialist in the area of low intensity conflicts and related fields and replace the State Department's Ambassador-at-Large for Counterterrorism as both the nation's chief antiterrorist official and a chairman of the Interdepartmental Group on Terrorism. He should also assume the chairmanship of the Senior Interdepartmental Group on Terrorism.

The creation of such an official and staff should ensure the continuity and consistency of the U.S. response to terrorism. There have been approximately 12 Acting Directors or Directors of the Department of State's Office for Counterterrorism and Emergency Planning—formerly the Office for Combating Terrorism and currently the Office of the Ambassador-at-Large for Counterterrorism—during the past 15 years. Their average tenure in office has been a little more than 12 months.[117] The constant rotation of these officials is a major weakness in the U.S. response to terrorism and is undermining its coordination and policy efforts. An official inside the Executive Office of the President would increase the continuity of U.S. efforts by not being rotated to another post just as he becomes experienced with the issue of terrorism.

Another major benefit of this organizational change should be the easing of the influence of bureaucratic behavior and the addressing of the dual-hat problem of the Ambassador-at-Large for Counterterrorism. The executive official, backed by presidential authority and unburdened with representing any department or agency with line functions and responsibilities, should have a greater degree of influence over the other actors involved in the antiterrorist bureaucracy. A criticism of the present structure is that the Ambassador's authority is being undermined by the fact that he is, on the one hand, the head of the Interdepartmental Group on Terrorism and is, on the other hand, the State Department's chief representative to the same organization. Because of the Ambassador's dual position, his ability to direct other officials is being undermined.

The proposed Office of the Deputy Assistant for National Security Affairs for Low-Intensity Conflicts' primary responsibility should be focused, in the words of Colonel John D. Waghelstein, an analyst with the U.S. Army War College's Strategic Studies Institute, on "the limited use of power for political purposes by nations or organizations . . . to coerce, control or defend a territory or establish or defend rights and military operations by or against irregular forces, peacekeeping operations, terrorism, counter-terrorism, rescue operations and military assistance under conditions of armed conflict."[118]

The Office for Low-Intensity Conflicts, as illustrated by chart 7, is conceived as a multiple-level organization consisting of nine administrative units and staffed by professionals drawn from both federal agencies and the private sector. The first level of organization is comprised of the Office of Global Insurgency. This office is designed to examine and evaluate trends in terrorism, guerrilla movements and Civil War/Wars of liberation and Soviet involvement in the Third World and its impact on U.S. national security. The office is headed by a senior analyst with the title of Director and is staffed with a Deputy Director and an analyst for the Middle East, Europe, Africa, Asia and Latin America. The Office for Global Insurgency chief

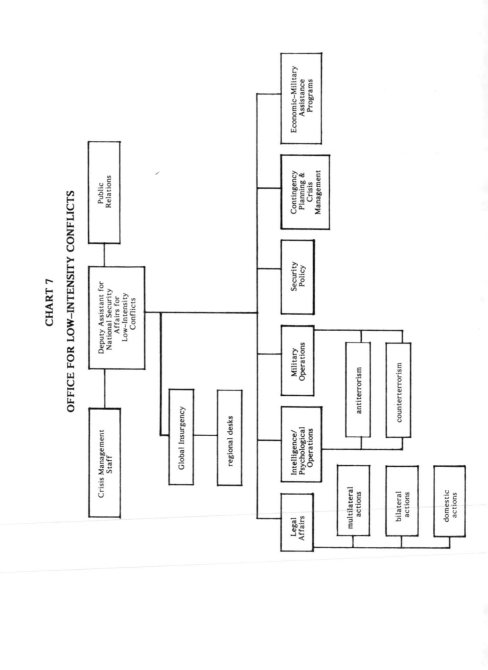

CHART 7

OFFICE FOR LOW-INTENSITY CONFLICTS

Public Relations

Deputy Assistant for National Security Affairs for Low-Intensity Conflicts

Crisis Management Staff

Global Insurgency

regional desks

Economic–Military Assistance Programs

Contingency Planning & Crisis Management

Security Policy

Military Operations

antiterrorism

counterterrorism

Intelligence/ Psychological Operations

Legal Affairs

multilateral actions

bilateral actions

domestic actions

task is to provide the Deputy Assistant with an independent source of information that is not tied to a department or agency with specific functional responsibilities so that he can participate within the interdepartmental arena with a greater degree of independence.

As illustrated by chart 8, the Deputy Assistant represents an important component in the planning, coordination and formulation of U.S. antiterrorist policy, with the second level of organization of the Office for Low-Intensity Conflicts representing the National Security Council's chief oversight mechanism. The office's oversight function is executed by six staffs that report directly to the Deputy Assistant. The six staffs oversee legal affairs, intelligence/psychological operations, security policy, military operations, contingency planning and crisis management and economic- and military-assistance programs that deal with unconventional conflicts. Each staff is assigned only an oversight and review responsibility.

The policy process demonstrated by the chart 8 begins with either a study request or policy decision by the National Security Council. The request or policy decision is handed to the National Security Adviser, who hands it to the Deputy Assistant for Low-Intensity Conflicts. The Deputy Assistant as chairman of the Senior Interdepartmental Group on Terrorism brings the NSC's action to the group, where the proper department(s) are chosen.

Through the Deputy Assistant, the departments and agencies of the Interdepartmental Group on Terrorism are informed of policy decisions and the units that have been assigned to fulfill study requests. Finally, the concerned department(s) and administrative unit(s) act to fulfill study requests and implement policy decisions. At the point that the organizations are informed of policy decisions or assigned study requests, the Deputy Assistant assigns and informs the proper oversight staff(s) within his office of the nature of the NSC's action and the organizations involved.

During the review process, option papers work their way up through the Interdepartmental Group and Senior Interdepartental Group. At both levels, a weeding-out process occurs in which by the conclusion of the Senior Group's review, only a select few papers remain. Before the Deputy Assistant presents the National Security Adviser and the National Security Council the Senior Group's recommendations, the oversight staffs are called on to comment on the recommendations. Once this stage is cleared, the recommendations or options are handed to the National Security Adviser and on to the National Security Council and the President for action.

The oversight staff's primary duty is to keep the Deputy Assistant informed of the progress in fulfilling study requests and how well policy decisions are being implemented. The goal of the Office for Low-Intensity Conflicts' oversight function is to enhance policy implementation. The implementation of policy decisions represents 20 percent of the policy process and is as important as the formulation of policy. Effective oversight is vital to the effectiveness of any policy.

The final two organizations comprising the Office for Low-Intensity Conflicts are its Public Relations and Crisis Management Staffs. The Public Relations unit is staffed by a public relations officer who is charged with fulfilling information requests from the Office of the National Security Adviser concerning the Office for Low-Intensity Conflicts' functions that are for public consumption.

Currently, the National Security Council heads the Terrorist Incident Working Group (TIWG), with the Vice President acting as the president's chief crisis manager. The TIWG is charged with the coordination of "agency response to specific

CHART 8

PROPOSED U.S. GOVERNMENT ORGANIZATION FOR ANTITERRORISM PLANNING, COORDINATION AND POLICY FORMULATION

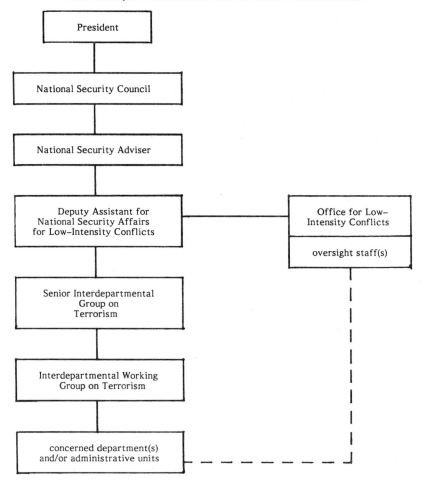

terrorist incidents, including the use of military forces."[119] The Vice President draws staff support from his own office. As illustrated by chart 9, the proposed Office of the Deputy Assistant for Low–Intensity Conflicts' Crisis Management staff, comprised of personnel from the Office of Global Insurgency and chaired by the Deputy Assistant, is designed to provide the Vice President with personnel and expertise in handling terrorist incidents. During a terrorist incident, the Deputy Assistant also heads the Interdepartmental Working Group on Terrorism and oversees its response and acts as the link between top policy makers and those lead agencies handling tactical matters.

The first task of the Office for Low–Intensity Conflicts, once it has been established, is the execution of an extensive study of unconventional problems, mainly terrorism. For the U.S. to deal effectively with the unconventional threats of the late–1980s and 1990s, it must understand these problems and cannot be caught seeking answers to these threats after they have already undermined and reduced American influence in key regions, like the Middle East and Latin America. Only a better understanding of these threats will equip the United States with the knowledge needed to compete on a level likely to produce success. The study should be divided into three sections examining short–term, mid–range and long–term trends in low–intensity conflicts. The short–term component of the study should examine the scope and range of low–intensity conflicts, mainly terrorism, during the next two years so as to outline the areas in which immediate actions are needed to protect U.S. interests and enhance the protection of American citizens traveling and living abroad. Next, the mid–range section should extend the examination of the scope and range of low–intensity conflicts into the late 1980s and early 1990s. This section of the study should seek to equip U.S. policy makers with the information needed to construct those programs that will enhance American national security. Finally, the long term should be designed to look at trends in low–intensity conflicts during the next 10 to 15 years, with the goal of making policy makers aware of projected threats to U.S. interests.

The goals of the above recommendations are to enhance interdepartmental and intradepartmental coordination efforts and to integrate the U.S. response to terrorism with that of other components of American foreign policy. The U.S. response to terrorism must be formulated with the goal of minimizing both the influence of domestic politics and the adverse aspects of bureaucratic behavior. On October 15, 1986, the Congress approved the "Fiscal Year 1987 National Defense Authorization Bill." Attached to the Bill was a provision sponsored by Senator William S. Cohen (R–Maine) calling for the reorganization of the Department of Defense's Special Forces. One aspect of the bill mandated the establishment within the National Security Council of a Board of Low–Intensity Conflict and "suggests that the President designate a Deputy Assistant for National Security Affairs for Low–Intensity Conflict."[120] This development is strongly supported and it is hoped that the recommended course of action is carried out.

CHART 9

PROPOSED U.S. GOVERNMENT ORGANIZATION FOR RESPONSE TO TERRORIST INCIDENTS

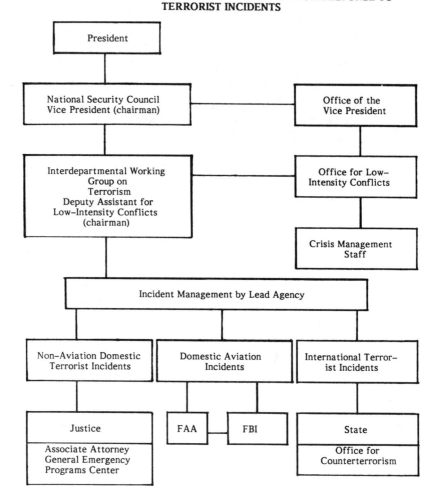

NOTES

1.   U.S. Department of State, *International Terrorism: Current Trends and the U.S. Response*, Bureau of Public Affairs Circular no. 706 (Washington, D.C.: U.S. Department of State, Bureau of Public Affairs, Office of Communications, May 1985), p. 3.

2.   U.S. Department of State, *Departmental Notice* (24 May 1984).

3.   U.S. Department of State, *International Terrorism*, Bureau of Public Affairs Circular no. 706, p. 4.

4.   U.S. Congress, House, Subcommittee on Civil and Constitutional Rights of the Committee on the Judiciary, *Federal Capabilities in Crisis Management and Terrorism*, 96th Cong., 2d sess., 19 May 1980, pp. 55–56.

5.   U.S. Department of State, *International Terrorism* (Washington, D.C.: Department of State GIST, September 1984).

6.   U.S. Department of State, *Combatting Terrorism: American Policy and Organization*, Department of State Bulletin (August 1982), p. 4.

7.   James A. Nathan, "The New Feudalism," in *Policy Choices: Critical Issues in American Foreign Policy*, ed. John Stack (Guilford, Conn.: Duskin Publishing Group, 1983), pp. 206–213.

8.   Ken Follett, *On Wings of Eagles* (New York: William Morrow and Company, 1983).

9.   Nathan, "New Feudalism," p. 209.

10. Ibid., p. 210.

11. U.S. Congress, "Anti–terrorism Program," *Congressional Quarterly*, April 2, 1983, p. 683.

12. U.S. Congress, House, Subcommittee on Arms Control, International Security and Science and on International Operations of the Committee on Foreign Affairs and the Subcommittee on Aviation of the Committee on Public Works and Transportation, *Joint Hearings: Impact of International Terrorism on Travel*, 99th Cong., 2d sess., 15 May 1986, p. 289.

13. Ibid.

14. Telephone Conversation with George Middleton, International Relations Officer, Office for Counter–terrorism and Emergency Planning, Department of State (632–9892), December 2, 1984.

15. U.S. Department of State, *Departmental Notice*.

16. U.S. Department of State, *Combatting Terrorism*, p. 6.

17. U.S Department of State, *Combatting International Terrorism*, Department of State Bulletin (June 1985), p. 75.

18. U.S. Department of State, *Combatting Terrorism*, p.2.

19. Ibid., p. 28.

20. Ibid.

21. Ibid.

22. Ibid.

23. Ibid.

24. Ibid., p. 29.

25. Ibid.

26. Ibid.

27. U.S. Congress, House, Subcommittee on Civil and Constitutional Rights of the Committee on the Judiciary, *Federal Capabilities in Crisis Management and Terrorism*, 95th Cong., 2d sess., 16 August 1978, p. 36.

28. ABC, "This Week with David Brinkley," 23 September 1984, show #152, David Brinkley, moderator, p. 8.

29. "Embassy Safety Gets Priority: Shultz Demands Daily Briefings on Progress," *The Washington Post*, 14 October 1984, p. A14.

30. "U.S. Tightening Embassy Security Worldwide," *The Washington Post*, 23 January 1985, p. A19.

31. U.S. Congress, "Hill Clears $2.4 Billion Project to Boost Security at Embassies," *Congressional Quarterly*, August 16, 1986, p. 1882.

32. U.S. Congress, Senate, Committee on Foreign Relations, *International Terrorism: Hearings on S. 873*, 97th Cong., 1st sess., 10 June 1981, p. 35.

33. U.S. Department of State, *Combatting Terrorism*, p. 6.

34. U.S. Congress, Senate, Committee on Governmental Affairs, *An Act to Combat International Terrorism: Hearings on S. 2236*, 95th Cong., 2d sess., 27 January 1978, pp. 129–131.

35. Charles W. Kegley, Jr., and Eugene R. Wittkopf, *American Foreign Policy: Pattern and Process* (New York: St. Martin's Press, 1982), p. 355.

36. *Report of the Secretary of State's Advisory Panel on Overseas Security*, Admiral Bobby Inman, USN (Ret.), Chairman (Washington, D.C.: U.S. Department of State, June 1985), p. 20. Hereafter cited as Inman Report.

37. Ibid., p. 22.

38. Ibid.

39. Ibid., pp. 22–23.

40. U.S. Congress, House, Subcommittee on International Operations of the Committee on Foreign Affairs, *Aftermath of the Achille Lauro Incident: Hearings on H. Con. Res. 228*, 99th Cong., 1st sess., 7 November 1985, p. 34. *See also* Appendix A.

41. U.S.Department of State, *Combatting Terrorism*, p. 14.

42. U.S. Department of State, *Digest of United States Practice in International Law, 1975* (Washington, D.C.: U.S. Governmental Printing Office, 1978), pp. 198–199.

43. Ibid.

44. John F. Murphy, "State Self-Help and Problems of Public International Law," in *Legal Aspects of International Terrorism*, ed. Alona E. Evans and John F. Murphy (Lexington, Mass.: Lexington Books, 1978), pp. 565–570.

45. Ibid., p. 567.

46. Ibid., p. 568.

47. Ibid., p. 569.

48. U.S. Department of State, *International Terrorism*, Bureau of Public Affairs Circular no. 706, p. 5.

49. William Regis Farrell, *The U.S. Government Response to Terrorism: In Search of an Effective Strategy* (Boulder, Colorado: Westview Press, 1982), p. 33.

50. Stephen D. Cohen, *The Making of United States International Economic Policy: Principles, Problems, and Proposals for Reform* (New York: Praeger Publishers, 1981), p. 18.

51. The 15 legislative acts are: (1) the Export Administration Act of 1979, (2) the Trade Act of 1974, (3) the Export Administration Act of 1969 (amended), (4) the Export–Import Bank Act of 1945, (5) the Foreign Assistance Act of 1961, (6) the International Security Assistance Act of 1977, (7) the Antihijacking Act of 1974, (8) the International Security and Development Cooperation Act of 1980, (9) Public Law 95–118, (10) the International Security and Development Cooperation Act of 1981,

(11) the Special Central American Assistance Act of 1979, (12) the Foreign Assistance Act of 1985, (13) the International Security and Development Cooperation Act of 1985, (14) the Foreign Assistance and Related Programs Appropriation Act of 1979, and (15) Omnibus Diplomatic Security and Anti–Terrorism Act of 1986.

52. U.S. Department of State, *International Terrorism*, Department of State Bulletin (August 1986), p. 3; idem,. *International Terrorism*, Bureau of Public Affairs Circular no. 706, p. 5.

53. U.S. Congress, Senate, Committee on Governmental Affairs, *Omnibus Antiterrorism Act of 1979: Hearings on S. 333*, 96th Cong., 1st sess., 30 March 1979, p. 70.

54. U.S. Congress, Senate, Committee on Foreign Relations, *International Terrorism: Hearings on S. 873*, p. 39.

55. U.S. Department of State, *President Nixon Establishes Cabinet Committee to Combat Terrorism*, Department of State Bulletin (October 23, 1972), p. 478.

56. U.S. Department of State, *United States Foreign Policy 1974: A Report of the Secretary of State* (Washington, D.C.: U.S. Government Printing Office, 1975), p. 92.

57. "Antiterrorist Program Faulted," *The Washington Post*, 6 March 1985, p. A8.

58. U.S. Department of State, *The Department of State Today*, Bureau of Public Affairs Circular, Bicentennial Notes no. 2, (Washington, D.C.: U.S. Department of State, Bureau of Public Affairs, Office of Public Communications, December 1980), p. 6.

59. I.M. Destler, *President, Bureaucrats, and Foreign Policy: The Politics of Organizational Reform* (Princeton, N.J.: Princeton University Press, 1974), p. 279.

60. Ibid.

61. Ibid., p. 280.

62. U.S. Department of State, *The Department of State Today*, p. 2.

63. John F. Murphy, "Report on Conference on International Terrorism: Protection of Diplomatic Premises and Personnel, Bellagio, Italy, March 8–12, 1982," *Terrorism: An International Journal* 6, no. 3 (1983): 488.

64. "Criticism of Security at Embassy Rises Probers Go to Beirut: State Dept. Disputes Charges of Laxity," *The Washington Post*, 22 September 1984, p. A1.

65. "GAO Found Delays in Security Improvements," *The Washington Post*, 30 September 1984, p. A27.

66. John M. Collins, *U.S. Defense Planning: A Critique* (Boulder, Colorado: Westview Press, 1982), p. 200.

67. U.S. Department of State, *International Terrorism*, Department of State Bulletin, p. 2.

68. Farrell, *The U.S. Government Response to Terrorism*, p. 104.

69. "Antiterrorist Command Post: It's Right Out of the Movies," *The New York Times*, 5 December 1984, p. A8.

70. U.S. Congress, Senate, Committee on Governmental Affairs, *An Act to Combat International Terrorism: Hearing on S. 2236*, 22 February 1978, p. 209.

71. Robert H. Kupperman and Darrell Trent, *Terrorism: Threat, Reality, Response* (Stanford, Calif.: Hoover Institution Press, 1979), p. 167.

72. "FBI Exhibits New Hostage Rescue Team," *The Washington Post*, 10 March 1984, p. A2.

73. U.S. Congress, Senate, Committee on Governmental Affairs, *An Act to Combat International Terrorism: Hearings on S. 2236*, 23 March 1978, p. 349.

74. Ibid., p. 39.

TERRORISM AND REAGAN POLICIES

75. "Antiterrorist Command Post: It's Right out of the Movies," *The New York Times*, 5 December 1984, p. A8.

76. U.S. Congress, Senate, Committee on Governmental Affairs, *An Act to Combat International Terrorism: Hearings on S. 2236*, 22 February 1978, p. 223.

77. Ibid., p. 233.

78. Patrick J. Montana and George S. Roukis, eds., *Managing Terrorism: Strategies for the Corporate Executive* (Westport, Conn.: Quorum Books, 1983), p. 146.

79. Ibid.

80. U.S. Congress, House, Subcommittee on Civil and Constitutional Rights of the Committee on the Judiciary, *Federal Capabilities in Crisis Management and Terrorism*, 96th Cong., 2d sess., 19 May 1980, p. 59.

81. Edward A. Lynch, "International Terrorism: The Search for a Policy," *Terrorism: An International Journal* 9, no. 1 (1987): 29–42.

82. U.S. Department of State, *International Terrorism*, Department of State Bulletin, p. 1.

83. Inman Report, p. 46.

84. U.S. Congress, House, Subcommittee on Arms Control, International Security and Science and on International Operations of the Committee on Foreign Affairs and the Subcommittee on Aviation of the Committee on Public Works and Transportations, *Joint Hearings: Impact of International Terrorism on Travel*, p. 34.

85. U.S. Congress, Senate, Committee on Governmental Affairs, *An Act to Combat International Terrorism: Hearings on S. 2236*, 25 January 1978, p. 54.

86. U.S. Congress, House, Subcommittee on Civil and Constitutional Rights of the Committee on the Judiciary, *Federal Capabilities in Crisis Management and Terrorism*, 19 May 1980, p. 51.

87. U.S., *Statutes at Large*, vol. 88, pt. 1.

88. U.S. Congress, Senate, Committee on Governmental Affairs, *An Act to Combat International Terrorism: Hearing on S. 2236*, 25 January 1978, p. 39.

89. U.S. Congress, House, Subcommittee on Civil and Constitutional Rights of the Committee on the Judiciary, *Federal Capabilities in Crisis Management and Terrorism*, 16 August 1978, p. 58.

90. Jan S. Breemer, "Offshore Energy Terrorism: Perspectives on a Problem," *Terrorism: An International Journal* 6, no. 3 (1983): 455–465.

91. Farrell, *The U.S. Government Response to Terrorism*, p. 101.

92. U.S. Congress, Senate, Committee on Governmental Affairs, *An Act to Combat International Terrorism: Hearings on S. 2236*, 22 February 1978, p. 200.

93. Ibid., p. 67.

94. Ibid., p. 68.

95. Ibid., p. 67. The information presented for the NRC was confirmed by a telephone conversation with the NRC on September 23, 1986: 1–200–492–7000.

96. Ibid., p. 337.

97. Ibid., p. 338.

98. John Frook, "Why They're Called 'Suicide Jockeys,'" *Parade Magazine* (July 3, 1983): 10. The information presented for Department of Energy was confirmed by a telephone conversation with Wolfegang Rosenberg of the Office of Assistance Secretary of Energy for Defense Programs on September 23, 1986: 1–202–252–1870.

99. U.S. President, Executive Order 12148, "Federal Emergency Management," *Weekly Compilation of Presidential Documents* 15, (July–September 1979); 1277–1284.

100. Kupperman and Trent, *Terrorism*, p. 175.

101. U.S. Department of State, *Combatting Terrorism*, p. 14.

102. U.S. Department of State, *Terrorist Attacks against U.S. Business* (Washington, D.C.: Office for Combatting Terrorism, June 1982, p. 1.

103. U.S. Congress, Senate, Committee on Governmental Affairs, *An Act to Combat International Terrorism: Hearings on S. 2236*, 23 January 1978, p. 7.

104. Edward F. Mickolus, *Transnational Terrorism: A Chronology of Events, 1968–1979* (Westport, Conn.: Greenwood Press, 1980), p. 394.

105. U.S. Congress, Senate, Committee on Foreign Relations, *Combatting International and Domestic Terrorism: Hearings on S. 2236*, 95th Cong., 2d sess., 8 June 1978, p. 70.

106. U.S. Congress, Senate, Committee on Governmental Affairs, *An Act to Combat International Terrorism: Hearings on S. 2236*, 22 February 1978, pp. 279–280.

107. U.S. Congress, Senate, Committee on Governmental Affairs, *Omnibus Antiterrorism Act of 1979: Hearings on S. 333*, 30 March 1979, p. 36.

108. U.S. Congress, House, Subcommittee on Civil and Constitutional Rights of the Committee on the Judiciary, *Federal Capabilities in Crisis Management and Terrorism*, 16 August 1978, p. 58.

109. U.S., *Statutes at Large*, vol. 91.

110. "Terrorist Policy: It Could Scare You to Death," *The Washington Post*, 15 February 1981, p. C4.

111. William J. Taylor, Jr., and Steven A. Maaranen, eds., *The Future of Conflict in the 1980s* (Lexington, Mass.: Lexington Books, 1982), p. 478.

112. Major General Donald R. Morelli, U.S. Army, (Ret.), and Major (P) Michael M. Ferguson, U.S. Army, "Low–Intensity Conflict: An Operational Perspective," *Military Review* (November 1984): 6.

113. James B. Motley, *U.S. Strategy to Counter Domestic Political Terrorism* (Washington, D.C.: National Defense University Press, 1983), p. 100.

114. Ibid.

115. U.S. Congress, Senate, Committee on Governmental Affairs, *An Act to Combat International Terrorism: Hearings on S. 2236*, 27 January 1978, p. 107.

116. Ibid.

117. See Appendix A.

118. Colonel John D. Waghelstein, U.S. Army, "Post–Vietnam Counterinsurgency Doctrine," *Military Review* (May 1985): 42.

119. Inman Report, p. 47.

120. Michael Gunley, "Congress Creates New Unified Command for SOF and New Civilian SOF Chief," *Armed Forces Journal International* (November 1986): 22.

5

U.S. Military Capabilities and Counterterrorism

A number of terrorist events have influenced the development of U.S. policy toward terrorism. Perhaps the most influential of these events was the October 23, 1983, truck bombing of the U.S. Marine barracks in Beirut and the April 5, 1986, bombing of the La Belle disco in West Berlin. The death of the 241 Marines in Beirut and U.S. Army Sergeant Kenneth Ford in West Berlin represent important stages of an intense debate within the Reagan administration over the means of combatting terrorism. The death of the Marines initiated this debate. While addressing the Trilateral Commission on April 3, 1984, Secretary of State Shultz presented one side of the debate by stating that "it is increasingly doubtful that a purely passive strategy can even begin to cope with the problem of terrorism. . . . it is more and more appropriate that the nations of the West face up to the need for an active defense against terrorism."[1]

Secretary Shultz's address corresponded with the same-day signing by President Reagan of National Security Decision Directive (NSDD) 138. The directive reportedly represents "a 'decision in principle' to use force against terrorism."[2] It orders "26 federal agencies and offices to provide President Reagan with options on how to implement the new policy."[3] It also reportedly seeks to coordinate intensified intelligence collection at home and abroad and promotes the creation and training of FBI and CIA paramilitary teams and Pentagon military squads.[4]

NSDD 138 represents, in the words of former Deputy Assistant Secretary of Defense Noel Koch, "a quantum leap in countering terrorism."[5] It signals the Reagan administration's desire to deter and prevent terrorism through the use of more unilateral methods as opposed to the multilateral, bilateral and unilateral steps used by past administrations. In addition, the signing of NSDD 138 signals a shift in the U.S. response to terrorism that began with Secretary of State Haig's statements in early 1981 that considered terrorism as a high-priority issue. The shifting nature of U.S. policy reached an important crossroad with the April 14, 1986, U.S. raid on Libya, in retaliation for the bombing of the La Belle disco. Whether the raid represents a one-time U.S. use of reprisals to counter terrorism or a permanent shift in policy still depends on the ongoing intra-administration debate on the use of force in implementing U.S. foreign policy and in combatting terrorism in particular. This debate is over what Philip Geyelin labeled the Shultz Doctrine.[6] It pits Secretary Shultz, an intense supporter of the use of force, against Vice President Bush, Defense Secretary Weinberger and the Joints Chiefs of Staff, all of whom are concerned with the use of force for unclear goals.[7] This chapter examines the role of military power in dealing with terrorism and the counterterrorism capabilities of the Department of Defense and U.S. Armed Services.

The Department of Defense (DOD) is the largest and one of the most active participants in the U.S. response to international terrorism. It has a comprehensive set of responsibilities and, in the light of the Reagan administration's consideration of forceful counterterrorist methods, a vital role. As outlined by the Inman Report, the DOD:

> performs substantial services in support of emergency planning for posts abroad and plays a lead role in executing such plans; provides expertise regarding terrorist weapons of all types, including nuclear and CBR; participates in collection, analysis and dissemination of intelligence regarding terrorist plans and activities; provides special units that might be called upon to intervene in terrorist episodes abroad; and generally manages security programs for military facilities abroad.[8]

The DOD deals with international terrorism within the context of its approach toward special operations. *Special operations*, as defined by the Joint Chiefs of Staff, are military operations "conducted by specially trained, equipped and organized forces against strategic or tactical targets in pursuit of national military, political, economic or psychological objectives" and "may be conducted during periods of peace or hostilities." In addition, they "may support conventional military operations, or they may be prosecuted independently when the use of conventional forces is inappropriate."[9] The Defense Department has been careful to demonstrate a division between its operations and "special activities" executed by the CIA. Former Deputy Assistant Secretary Koch has stated "that special activities are intelligence activities that are covert and designed for plausible denial by the U.S. as opposed to special operations, which whether overt or clandestine, are military operations which, if discovered, are acknowledged as U.S. activities."[10] The DOD's desire to separate its operation from those of the CIA extends from Secretary Weinberger's desire to separate and distinguish military operations and objectives from unclear political goals and comes from the hope of avoiding the type of Congressional apprehension that has plagued recent CIA special activities. The foundation of the department's behavior is based on National Security Action Memorandum 57, formulated by the Kennedy administration in response to the Bay of Pigs debacle, which stated "that whenever a secret paramilitary operation became so large and overt that the military contribution, in terms of manpower and equipment, exceeded the resources contributed by the CIA, the operation should be turned over to the DOD."[11]

Within the Office of the Secretary of Defense there is no single official or office that has total control over the department's special operations programs. The Office of the Assistant Secretary for International Security Affairs (ISA), through the Principal Deputy Assistant Secretary, "is the Office of the Secretary of Defense's focal point for special operations matters" in general and is charged with planning, coordinating and overseeing the department's counterterrorism program.[12]

In addition, the Deputy Assistant Secretary for ISA heads the department's Special Planning Directorate, "which is responsible for DOD policy on terrorism, counterterrorism and special operations, including strategic planning and doctrinal and force development" and the Defense Working Group on Terrorism.[13] The working group consists of representatives from the Office of the Secretary of

Defense, the Joint Chiefs of Staff, the Joint Special Operations Agency and Defense Intelligence Agency and the Secretary of Defense's Special Assistant for Atomic Energy. It is designed, as in the 1970s, "to focus on the problem of terrorism and to make recommendations to the Secretary on policies and procedures to counter terrorist threats."[14]

Oversight for special-operations forces resources is the responsibility of the Office of the Deputy Under Secretary for Command, Control, Communications and Intelligence (C^3I). This office's specific duties, executed by the Assistant Secretary for C^3I, currently Donald C. Latham, are "the oversight of reprogramming requests for special operations, oversight of equipment acquisition, research and development, and resource guidance in the Defense Guidance."[15] The Office of the Under Secretary for Policy represented by the Deputy Under Secretary, as outlined by former Deputy Assistant Secretary Koch, "is responsible for policy, departmental and interagency coordination, and advice to the Under Secretary, Deputy Secretary and Secretary of Defense on executive order 12333 'special matters.'"[16] In addition, the Under Secretary for Policy is the department's senior representative to the Senior Interdepartmental Group on Terrorism with the Office of the Assistant Secretary for ISA representing the department on the Interdepartmental Group on Terrorism.[17]

The DOD's military response to international terrorism is under the direction of the Joint Chiefs of Staff. The main components of the Armed Services' anti- and counterterrorist program consists of the Joint Chiefs of Staff/Joint Special Operations Agency, the Joint Special Operations Command, the services' intelligence units and the Defense Intelligence Agency. All U.S. military operations are designed for dealing with terrorists outside the United States. All paramilitary operations inside the United States fall under the jurisdiction of the FBI. The Armed Services are prohibited by law from engaging in domestic paramilitary operations. However, if a situation occurs requiring the use of Armed Services personnel, the President has the authority to waive statutory restrictions on such operations.[18]

One of the most important tools a nation can employ in dealing with terrorism is an effective military response. Richard H. Shultz, a Research Associate with the National Strategy Information Center has presented two uses of military force in combatting terrorism. The first is "to rescue U.S. citizens caught up in another nation's civil strife."[19] The second is "antiterrorist operations to rescue hostages, preempt the destruction of important facilities or resources, or retake them from the terrorists."[20]

Before the capture of the Achille Lauro hijackers in October 1985 and the April 14, 1986, raid on Libya, terrorism was handled by the United States as an unconventional threat to be dealt with by specially trained antiterrorist units. However, recent U.S. actions raise the possibility of using more conventional means to deal with terrorism, specifically state terrorism. Conventional actions, mainly retaliatory strikes, by Israel and South Africa, however, have never proven an effective means of deterring, preventing and suppressing terrorism. Although the impact of the U.S. attack on Libya is difficult, in terms of long-range terrorist activity, to judge, conventional actions do not offer a suitable solution to international terrorism. The capture of the Achille Lauro hijackers was a successful conventional antiterrorist action because of very unique circumstances. The U.S. Navy was able to track the terrorists' movements with a great deal of accuracy, thus ensuring their interception and subsequent capture. This type of intelligence is normally not available to a nation.

On the other hand, the raid on Libya, although supported by the American public, only raised the likelihood of a new wave of terrorism and witnessed the United States engaging in behavior that it has traditionally opposed. Instead of weakening Colonel Khaddafi, the raid may have fortified him both internally and within the Arab community. Although the moderate Arab states, such as Egypt and Saudi Arabia, may oppose Khaddafi, they are part of the Arab community and must oppose any attack on a fellow Arab state as a matter of solidarity, if not survival from internal radical elements. In addition, the harming of Khaddafi's family, because of the Arab need to protect honor and save face, alone could promote continued terrorist behavior. In the end, retaliatory strikes are a demonstration of a nation's frustration with a problem it cannot handle. Instead of deterring, preventing and suppressing terrorism, retaliatory raids only contribute to the escalatory and vicious cycle of strike and counterstrike. Finally, if retaliatory strikes are an effective means of combatting terrorism, one should ask why Israel carries out so many and why it invaded Lebanon in the summer of 1982?

The solution, if there is one, to states supporting terrorism is the use of special operations or activities that will cause these regimes, like Khaddafi's, to collapse due to their own internal weaknesses. Special foreign policy actions, such as those used against Allende in Chile during the mid-1970s, offer a viable solution to states supporting terrorism, and "presidents of both parties," as outlined by Henry Kissinger, "have felt the need for covert operations in the gray area between formal diplomacy and military intervention throughout the postwar period."[21]

As demonstrated by the Israeli Entebbe rescue operation and Italy's rescue of General James B. Dozier, an effective antiterrorist military capability presents a decision-maker with a viable policy option. The Israeli General Intelligence and Reconnaissance Unit 269, West Germany's Border Protection Group Nine (GSG-9) and Great Britain's 22nd Special Air Services Regiment have all been successful in demonstrating their effective capabilities in combatting terrorism.

For the United States to succeed in preventing, deterring and responding effectively to international terrorism, it must develop capabilities comparable to those of its allies. Unfortunately, the U.S. record in executing commando-style raids similar to Israel's Entebbe raid has been disappointing. The Son Tay raid, the Mayaguez affair and the Iranian rescue mission are clear examples of American disappointments, and as pointed out by Benjamin F. Schemmer, editor of the *Armed Forces Journal*, "except in the Civil War, despite scores of tries, there had never been a successful rescue of an American prisoner from a POW camp during all the years of America's military history."[22]

By the late 1970s, an estimated 14 nations had established commando units. In addition to those mentioned above, they were Belgium, Denmark, Italy, the Netherlands, Norway, France, Switzerland, Austria, Egypt and Indonesia.[23] Many of these nations formulated their commando units in the early 1970s in response to the growing occurrence of terrorism. However, due to the lack of a public perception of terrorism as a serious threat, the United States did not formulate its own antiterrorist program until 1977. Responding to mounting pressure from the media and Congress, in light of Israel's successful Entebbe operation and West Germany's Mogadishu operation, the Carter administration in the spring of 1977 announced the creation of an antiterrorist commando unit.[24]

On February 22, 1978, while appearing before the Senate's Committee on Governmental Affairs, Assistant Secretary of Defense for ISA David E. McGiffert outlined the American counterterrorist force structure and capabilities. The Assistant Secretary pointed out no single counterterrorism unit but instead presented a force structure consisting of more than 31 separate units, in which a selected group—mainly U.S. Army Ranger battalions, US Army Special Force (Green

Berets), Navy SEALS and Marine Corps Reconnaissance Teams—maintained a capacity to conduct counterterrorism operations. In addition, the Assistant Secretary stated that the "Joint Chiefs of Staff have developed plans to provide for U.S. military operations ranging from the rescue of hostages from a hijacked U.S. aircraft to the recovery/neutralization/destruction of stolen nuclear weapons." Finally, he made it clear that "each terrorist incident involving the United States overseas must be analyzed to determine if a military response would be appropriate and effective," and "depending on the nature of the mission, the size of U.S. military forces may range from a small element to a larger task force."[25]

Throughout the 1970s, the U.S. Army Ranger battalions (Black Berets) were considered the Armed Services' unit most likely to be used to handle a counterterrorism operation. Lieutenant Colonel Edward Yaugo, commander of the 1st Ranger Battalion during the mid-1970s, has stated that "if we had an Entebbe of our own and the Army didn't call on us, we'd be pretty damned mad. We are the cream of the Army. The Entebbe thing is just what we're trained to do."[26] However, doubts existed about the quality of the Black Berets' counterterrorist training. Neil C. Livingstone, Director of Terrorism and Low-Level Warfare at the American Security Council, pointed out that "many observers during the 1970s doubted the Black Berets effectiveness since, on the whole, their training program emphasized traditional military skills and techniques more suitable to combat conditions than to counterterrorism operations."[27]

The force structure outlined by Assistant Secretary McGiffert, along with the lack of the proper counterterrorist skills on the part of the Black Berets, represented the unprepared nature of the United States during the mid-1970s to handle terrorism and demonstrated the services' inability to address the issue with a unified and effective effort. The first truly determined effort by the Armed Services to formulate a counterterrorist unit began on November 9, 1977, with the activation of the Fort Bragg-based, 200-man 1st Special Forces Operational Detachment Delta (Delta Force), under the command of Colonel Charles A. Beckwith.[28] Although Delta Force was activated on November 9, 1977, it was not operational for another two years. As a stop-gap measure, General Jack Mackmull, then commander of the JFK Center for Military Assistance, after a meeting with General Jack Hennessey, then commander of the Readiness Command (REDCOM), ordered Colonel Bob Mountel to establish a temporary counterterrorism unit made up of personnel from the 5th Special Forces Group, which Colonel Mountel personally codenamed "Blue Light."[29]

General Hennessey and REDCOM, under a 1976 counterterrorism contingency plan, were responsible for the testing and transportation of counterterrorist units "from the continental U.S. to the various unified command areas located throughout the world."[30] The 1976 contingency plan authorized General Hennessey to call on General Mackmull to provide a unit to combat a terrorist incident occurring within and involving REDCOM's jurisdictional responsibilities. To fulfill this possible task, General Mackmull ordered the setting up of a stop-gap solution—"Blue Light." The establishment, however, of Blue Light and the activation of Delta Force triggered an intense intraservice and intraunit power struggle. Instead of acting as a short-term solution, Colonel Mountel and Blue Light, backed by major officers of the Army's Special Forces and other units, attempted to block the development of Delta Force. The debate of which unit, Blue Light or Delta Force, would be the U.S. Army's chief counterterrorism unit continued until August 7, 1978, at which time Army Deputy Chief of Staff General Edward Meyer, under pressure from the Joint Chiefs and President Carter, put an end to the conflict by backing Delta Force while attending a briefing at Fort Bragg on the status of the service's counterterrorist capabilities.[31]

The November 4, 1979, Iranian seizure of the U.S. Teheran Embassy offered the United States its first opportunity to demonstrate its newly formulated counterterrorism capabilities. On November 6, 1979, President Carter ordered the preparations and planning for a rescue operation to proceed.[32] By April 1980, Delta Force and other units taking part in the rescue operation were ready, and on April 11, 1980, President Carter authorized Operation Eagle Claw, which began and ended tragically on April 24, 1980, on the desert sands of Iran.

This operation, like all hostage–rescue missions, was a high–risk political–military venture that pushed to the edge what was technologically and humanly possible. Unfortunately, Operation Eagle Claw pushed U.S. military capabilities to the breaking point. Why the mission failed has been credited by a number of analysts––such as Schlomo Gazit, former Director of Israeli Military Intelligence; Richard A. Gabriel, former U.S. Army Intelligence officer; Gary Sick, former Carter administration National Security Council (NSC) staff member for Iran and others––to a variety of factors ranging from a flawed planning structure that did not allow for competitive planning and critical review to excessive security precautions that maintained surprise but undermined the integration, coordination and training of the various components of the mission to poor weather conditions and the lack of helicopters to bad luck.

The failure of Operation Eagle Claw led in the early 1980s to the conclusion by a number of analysts that U.S. "forces, to deter or defeat either sophisticated operations by professional terrorists or for larger–scale, unconventional–warfare operations, are inadequate."[33] It is doubtful "that the U.S. military really grasps counter–insurgency even today, nor do we have a counterinsurgency doctrine or assets."[34] The lessons of the rescue mission were that the United States was, and still is, physically and psychologically unprepared to deal with terrorism.

In executing and formulating rescue operations, there exist numerous variables that must be incorporated into a plan, variables such as assessment, speed, security, command, control, communications, transportation, force selection and training.[35] It is important to recognize that the success of Great Britain, West Germany and Israel in executing counterterrorism operations derives from their ability to understand these components and their recognition of the importance each one of the variables plays in an effective operation. These nations have established permanent counterterrorism organizations, which has granted their units the time and resources needed to study effectively the terrorist threat. However, the United States has handled the issue on an ad hoc basis. Colonel Beckwith cited this as a major fault of the Iranian rescue mission in particular and the U.S. terrorism program in general.[36]

In response to the failure of Operation Eagle Claw, Army Chief of Staff General Meyer accepted a plan by Colonel Beckwith, in the late spring of 1980, establishing the Joint Special Operations Command (JSOC). The JSOC represents the military's chief counterterrorist operational organization and is designed to unify and coordinate the training of the services' different counterterrorism units.[37] It is made up of 30 special operations units, with Delta Force, supported by the 160th Aviation Battalion ('Night Stalkers'), and Navy SEAL units being the central components. The JSOC is stationed at Fort Bragg, and its first commander was Major General Richard A. Scholtes.

In addition to the creation of the JSOC, the failure of the hostage rescue mission led to the establishment of a review group, under the chairmanship of Admiral James L. Holloway. Operating with a limited mandate, the Holloway Group's, as pointed out by Paul B. Ryan, a Research Fellow at Stanford University's Hoover Institution on War, Revolution and Peace, "sole purpose was to ascertain those operational and material deficiencies in need of modification for future operations."[38] The Holloway Group concluded its first review during August 1980 and made two recommendations. The first stated that there "should be established a field agency of the Joint Chiefs of Staff with a permanently assigned staff and certain assigned forces" designed as a counterterrorism task force providing "the president with many options, ranging from a small group of highly trained specialists to a large joint force."[39] Acting on this recommendation, Secretary of Defense Brown set up the Counterterrorist Joint Task Force (CTJTF), The CTJTF, between October 1984 and January 1984, executed the operational oversight of and planning for the JSOC.

Acting on the Holloway Group's second recommendations, the DOD established the Special Operations Advisory Panel. The panel was designed as a review group consisting of independent and impartial active and retired senior officers, so as to provide an objective and critical review and approval of missions. In a move to incorporate the panel's review procedures into the DOD, it was, on December 20, 1983, reconstituted as the Special Operations Policy Advisory Group (SOPAG). The SOPAG's review responsibilities were extended to deal with key policy issues relating to all areas of special operations.[40]

In an effort to increase U.S. special operations capabilities, the Reagan administration incorporated into the Defense Guidance of 1981 an order to the Armed Services to develop special–operations capabilities.[41] On March 4, 1983, Secretary of the Army John Marsh, in a keynote address to a two–day symposium, The Role of Special Operations in U.S. Strategy for the 1980s, stated that the Defense Guidance of 1981 is significant in that the term *special operations* was for the first time used in an official document and that "it clearly incorporates special operations into national strategy."[42]

During the early 1980s, a U.S. counterterrorism organization was cited as "capable of responding to any future incidents that may occur."[43] While appearing before a conference on international terrorism on March 8–12, 1982, in Bellagio, Italy, General Volney F. Warner (Ret.) "spoke of efforts in the U.S. and elsewhere to develop an elite counterterrorist option" and pictured American capabilities as adequate.[44]

On October 1, 1982, in a move to coordinate and enhance the U.S. Army's Special Operation Forces (SOFs), in light of the Reagan administration's attempts to rebuild American special forces in response "to threats at the lower end of the spectrum," the 1st Special Operations Command was activated.[45] The 1st Special Operations Command, as outlined by Major General Robert L. Schweitzer, Director, Strategic Plans and Policy Directorate, has provided the Army's SOFs with "more coordinated training, contingency planning, doctrine, logistic support and command and control." He has outlined the command as the Army's single spokesman for special forces, which "will help in the competition for resources and research and development."[46] Acting along the same lines, the U.S. Air Force combined its SOFs with its Combined Rescue units under the 23rd Air Force.[47]

Two events in 1983, however, call into question General Warner's remarks and the impact that the increased interest has had on improving U.S. Special Forces and raise doubts about the Armed Services' abilities to understand and respond to crisis situations and terrorism. In response to an unstable and threatening situation on the island of Grenada, the United States on October 25, 1983, through Operation Urgent Fury, invaded the island. Operation Urgent Fury has been labeled a military success. However, an analysis of the Grenada invasion by the Military Reform Institute for the Congressional Military Reform Caucus has outlined a number of failures—such as the Richmond Hill prison incident—by units of the JSOC taking part in the invasion. The institute's report states:

> Delta Force personnel were brought in to take Richmond Hill prison. They attempted to do the job by landing near the prison, by helicopter, in daylight. Hostile forces in or near the prison took the helicopter under fire and drove it off, inflicting casualties on our troops. Delta then repeated exactly the same tactics with another helicopter the next day! The result was predictable: they were again driven off, with casualties, this time by a force of just three Grenadian prison guards. Subsequently, the prison was taken by some newsmen who walked through the front door and discovered that the guards had decamped.[48]

This event raises doubts about the ability of the United States to conceptualize and implement an effective operation on short notice and has led Richard A. Gabriel to state "that the creation of JSOC after the Iran debacle has done little to improve the ability of U.S. forces to conduct commando operations, at least if the operations in Grenada are any test."[49] The ability to respond quickly to a terrorist incident with an effective operation is very important in determining the deterrence value of a nation's counterterrorist unit. If the United States continues to demonstrate a lack of ability to carry out effective operations, it undermines the deterrence value of its antiterrorist program. In addition, U.S. troops must be able to adapt to changing combat conditions. Nothing is predictable when combatting terrorism, and quick adjustments in a plan have to be anticipated.

Besides demonstrating a lack of combat skills, the Richmond Hill incident, along with the failure of the Iranian hostage mission, illustrates a lack of leadership. Colonel Harry G. Summer, U.S. Army, a strategist with the Army's Strategic Studies Institute, in a review of Colonel Charlie A. Beckwith's and Donald Knox's *Delta Force: America's Counterterrorist Unit and the Mission to Rescue the Hostages in Iran*, has questioned the Army's selection of Colonel Beckwith to lead the assault on the U.S. Embassy in Tehran. Using passages from *Delta Force*, Colonel Summers illustrated Colonel Beckwith's explosive character and lack of leadership once "the whole plan began to unravel" at Desert One. He concluded that the Army could have appointed a better commander to lead the rescue mission, and "the problem is that the Army is looking for boldness," not the ability on the part of officers to handle von Clausewitz's friction of war and command responsibilities.[50]

Unfortunately, the Richmond Hill incident shows a continued lack of leadership qualities, mainly imagination. Executing the same tactic that initially failed shows a lack of resourcefulness and flexibility that have been hallmarks of the U.S. Armed Services' officer corps. The above incidents outline a lack of combat skills and leadership that have proven tragic and if not corrected can do so again.

The second important and tragic event of 1983 is the October 23, 1983, terrorist attack on the Marines in Beirut. This incident raises doubts about the U.S. Armed Services' preparedness to deal with terrorism and the DOD's understanding of it. The Long Commission's report on the October 23 incident has outlined a number of general and specific problems with the U.S. response to terrorism and has made a number of recommendations. First, the report's executive summary declares that the incident "underscores the fact that terrorism can have significant political impact and demonstrates that the U.S., and specifically the Department of Defense, is inadequately prepared to deal with this threat." It concludes by stating that "much needs to be done, on an urgent basis, to prepare U.S. military forces to defend against and counter terrorist warfare."[51]

The Long Commission on a more specific level has concluded and recommended that "state sponsored terrorism is an important part of the spectrum of warfare and that adequate response to this increasing threat requires an active national policy which seeks to deter attack or reduce its effectiveness" and that policy must be "supported by political, diplomatic and timely military capabilities." To deal with terrorism, the commission recommended "that the Secretary of Defense directs the Joint Chiefs of Staff to develop a broad range of appropriate military responses to terrorism for review, along with political and diplomatic actions, by the National Security Council." In addition, the commission has concluded that U.S. forces were "not trained, organized, staffed or supported to deal effectively with the terrorist threat in Lebanon" and "that much needs to be done to prepare them to defend against and counter terrorism." To address the lack of preparedness of the military, "the Commission recommended that the Secretary of Defense direct the development of doctrine, planning, organization, force structure, education and training necessary to defend against and counter terrorism."[52]

The Long Commission report and the analysis done by the Military Reform Institute illustrate a number of weaknesses in the U.S. handling of terrorism. In an attempt to revitalize U.S. Special Forces capabilities and address some of the problems with the military's counterterrorist capacity, Deputy Secretary of Defense Paul Thayer, in the fall of 1983, issued a directive aimed at increasing resources and attention paid to SOFs.[53] As a part of the revitalization of Special Forces, the Joint Chiefs of Staff on January 1, 1984, formally established the Joint Special Operations Agency (JSOA).[54]

The JSOA, formulated as an alternative to the U.S. Army's proposed Strategic Services Command and the U.S. Air Forces' proposal for a Joint Command Agency, represents the military's desire to deal with terrorism and other unconventional threats by a joint approach and, as pointed out by former Deputy Assistant Secretary Koch, "was developed because of the lack of integration of doctrine, understanding of roles and missions, procurement, exercises . . . that have to be married together for effective operations."[55] It "is charged with," as stated by General Wesley Rice, USMC, first Director, JSOA, "advising the JCS in all matters pertaining to special operations and the military activities related thereto, including national strategy, planning, programming, budgeting, resource development and allocation, joint doctrinal guidance, exercise and readiness evaluating and employment of forces."[56] As illustrated by Chart 10, the JSOA is made up of a number of units, with the Research and Development and Acquisition (RD&A) Division and the Special Operations Division/Contingency Operations Branch being the chief units dealing with terrorism. The RD&A Division, as outlined by General Rice, "is charged with the responsibility of insuring that a capability exists in service and Office of the Secretary of Defense (OSD)/JCS programs to provide the rapid reaction acquisition or development of items required in special operations to include anti- and counterterrorism, unconventional warfare, psychological operations, and direct action activities."[57] The Special Operations Division/Contingency Operations Branch is the Joint Chiefs of Staff's main office for combatting terrorism. It is responsible for the analysis, coordination and standardization of "all aspects of exercises, training procedures and tactics for counterterrorism forces and evaluates JSOC programs and activities to insure adherence to national guidance and policy."[58]

Currently, the JSOA is headed by Major General Thomas W. Kelly, USA, and, once fully operational, will reportedly consist of 41 officers, 10 enlisted men and 10 civilians.[59] The JSOA reports directly to the Joint Chiefs of Staff, with the Director of Joint Staff charged with the monitoring and coordination of JSOA activities. It does not have command authority over the Joint Special Operations Command and its units.

CHART 10

JSOA ORGANIZATIONAL STRUCTURE

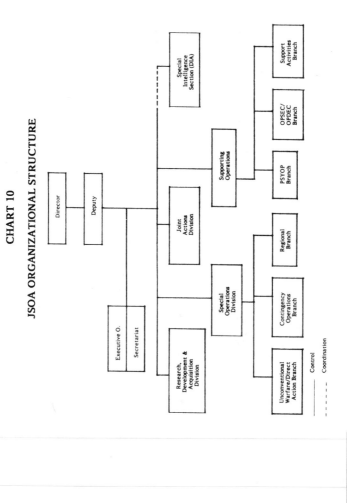

Control

- - - - - **Coordination**

Source: U.S. Congress, House, Subcommittee on the Department of Defense of the Committee on Appropriations, *Department of Defense Appropriations for 1985: Special Operations Forces*, 98th Cong., 2d sess., 10 April 1984, p. 803.

Note: PSYOP = Psychological Operations; OPSEC/OPDES = Operational Security/Deception Branch.

Besides conducting rescue operations, the Armed Services also perform a number of other important antiterrorist functions. The first function is the execution of counterintelligence operations. Following the conclusion of the Iranian hostage operation, the need for current and accurate intelligence became clear if the United States was to deal effectively with terrorism. Yet the U.S. military still lacks adequate intelligence capabilities. The Long Commission report states that "the U.S. Marine Corps commander did not have effective U.S. Human Intelligence (HUMINT) support and the lesson of Beirut is that we must have better HUMINT to support military planning and operations."[60] The exact role of intelligence and counterintelligence operations in combatting terrorism is outlined in the next chapter.

Another vital function of the Armed Services is dealing with nuclear terrorism. The services represent the DOD's operational arm in this area. However, the services' role is supportive in relation to those of other agencies dealing with nuclear terrorism. R. William Mengel, Director, Washington Operations, of the BDM Corporation, lists four Armed Services' duties. The first is the "planning for the prevention of, and response to, theft or sabotage of nuclear weapons under its control, coordinating with the Department of Energy, FBI and other agencies in responding to an incident, and facilitating the FBI investigative activities with respect to the theft or sabotage of weapons under its control." Their next duty is to develop "operational response to the detonation or widespread contamination from a nuclear weapon or materials under DOD control which does not involve major property damage and poses little threat to the general public." In addition, the Armed Services are required to "support other government agencies as authorized by law and as requested by those agencies." Finally, they are required to "respond to Presidential direction under the constitution and statutory authority in domestic disasters."[61]

The Armed Services' final function in combatting terrorism involves psychological operations (PSYOPS). Schlomo Gazit and Michael Handel, a member of Harvard University's Center for International Affairs, have stated that "psychological warfare is a powerful weapon in the war against terrorism. Its aim is to hit the terrorist organization at its most vulnerable spot—the motivation of its members and the readiness of others to join its ranks or to remain and operate within its framework."[62] The use of PSYOPS also represents a vital ingredient in the formulation and implementation of a rescue operation. PSYOPS, as pointed out by William J. Taylor, Jr., Director of political-military studies at Georgetown University's Center for Strategic and International Studies, provide a government with three vital functions: "to prepare the public and the enemy for the operation; to exploit the operation's success; and to explain or exploit, the best way possible, an operation's failure."[63] Unfortunately, the U.S. Army, the Armed Service responsible for the formulation and implementation of PSYOPS, throughout the early 1980s has been unprepared to carry out its responsibility. During this time, the Army has had only a part-time officer assigned to the Joint Chiefs of Staff and only four, grossly understaffed, field units dealing with PSYOPS.[64]

Presently, through the JSOA's Supporting Operations Division/Psychological Branch, the Armed Services have attempted to address some of the problems associated with PSYOPS. The PSYOPS Branch, as outlined by General Rice, "serves as the organization of the Joint Chiefs of Staff point of contact for psychological operations matters in the development of joint policy, tactics and training" and also "coordinates directly with the services, CINCs and DOD agencies proposed PSYOPS programs, force strategy, war plans and near-term force readiness."[65] The U.S. Army, currently, has 12 PSYOPS battalions.[66] According to the JSOA's Joint

Manpower Program for fiscal year 1984, the PSYOPS branch consists of three officers and one enlisted man.[67]

During the past five years, the Reagan administration has sought to increase the size and prestige of U.S. SOFs by institutionalizing "the revitalization process; and advancing the effort by persuasion, education, increasing the visibility of the SOF concept, and creating a public presumption that SOF must and will be restored."[68] By fiscal year 1990, the Reagan administration seeks to increase U.S. SOFs force structure by 50 percent over fiscal year 1981 levels and have 15 Army and 8 Navy SOF units established.[69]

Despite the increased public attention being paid to Special Forces, the current administration's awareness of their importance in dealing with terrorism and numerous steps to enhance the strength, prestige and coordination of efforts, doubts still exist concerning their abilities and the level of interest within the military for special operations. Pessimism over the Armed Services' interest in SOFs, as presented by Edward N. Luttwak, Senior Fellow, Georgetown University's Center for Strategic and International Studies, extends from the belief that "a military establishment primarily focused on administration, bureaucracy, major weapons-system acquisitions, management and office politics can only regard commando activities as deviant."[70]

Lending support to the phrase "the more things change, the more they stay the same" is an article by Deborah G. Meyer, senior editor of *Armed Forces Journal*, entitled "Four Years Later: Desert One Revisited?" appearing in the August 1985 issue of the journal. Deborah Meyer reported that like the Carter administration during the Iranian hostage mission, the Reagan administration during the TWA 847 incident was "unable to mount a hostage rescue because of rotary-wing deficiencies." Meyer charged that because of the lack of crews qualified to fly night missions assigned to the 67th Air Rescue and Recovery Squadron stationed at Woodbridge, England, the Reagan administration lacked a timely military option. At the same time that the Joint Chiefs of Staff were looking for a military option, the 67th Squadron was the only unit equipped with the helicopters required to perform a rescue operation that was available. The Joint Chiefs of Staff have cited the lack of trained crews as "a moot point" in regard to their planning of a rescue mission.[71] However, if Meyer's charges are corroborated, serious questions still exist relating to the DOD's capabilities.

Before discussing the obstacles facing the United States in developing a viable counterterrorism capability, it is important to state that the use of force in dealing with terrorism should be viewed as a last resort. The Reagan administration's stress on military solutions, as demonstrated by the raid on Libya, has distorted the proper role of force in combatting terrorism and what type of actions are truly effective. As outlined by Deputy Secretary of State John Whitehead, the administration sought to achieve three objectives in its use of force against Libya. The first was to demonstrate to Khaddafi that his continued support of terrorism "would not be without direct cost to Libya." The second objective was to demonstrate "that the United States was prepared to use force to fight terrorism along lines repeatedly and carefully defined by the President," and finally, the United States reserved "the right to defend itself and its citizens against aggression by any state, even when that aggression takes new forms, such as terrorism."[72] The United States, like all nations, has the right, if not the obligation, to protect itself and its citizens from any form of aggression. However, international terrorism is a political phenomenon that is not amenable to conventional military means. It is a low-level threat that should be initially dealt with by all diplomatic, political and economic means available, and only when these things are exhausted should military options be considered. When military options are considered, the goal of not escalating the importance of terrorism should be the operation's primary focus. Conventional military actions attract a large degree of attention and in the end distort the degree to which terrorism is a threat to U.S. national security.

When military action is needed, special operations, as outlined by Maurice Tugwell, Director, Center for Conflict Studies, University of New Brunswick, and David Charters, Deputy Director, Center for Conflict Studies, University of New Brunswick, offer a viable and vital solution to terrorism. The Joint Chiefs of Staff's definition of *special operations*, outlined earlier, has been criticized because it is too narrowly focused on military means to be effective. Maurice Tugwell's and David Charter's definition is more useful in dealing with unconventional problems and describes *special operations* as "small-scale, clandestine, covert or overt operations of an unorthodox and frequently high-risk nature, undertaken to achieve significant political or military objectives in support of foreign policy." These "operations are characterized by either simplicity or complexity, by subtlety and imagination, by the discriminate use of violence and by oversight at the highest levels."[73]

It is important to state, however, that the use of military force is not an adequate alternative to an effective foreign policy. If military actions are executed to deal with unconventional threats, the United States should, as outlined by William V. O'Brien, Professor of Government, Georgetown University, "observe the highest practicable standards of just war and international law irrespective of the legal status of participants in or victims of the conflict."[74]

The foundation of many of the obstacles to the formulation of effective U.S. SOFs is the traditional military dislike for anything that is unconventional, irregular and elite. Top U.S. Army commanders have seen Special Forces, at best, as a cost-effective way to inflict losses and discomfort on the enemy and at worst as "a crackpot 'non-Army' method of fighting a war."[75] The traditional military perceptive, as stated by Roger M. Pezzelle, former Chief, Special Operations Division, J–3 (Operations), Organization of the Joint Chiefs of Staff, is "that any good infantryman will make a good special forces soldier."[76] An illustration of Pezzelle's statement is the appointment in the spring of 1986 of Army Major General Thomas W. Kelly to the Directorship of the JSOA. Major General Kelly is a specialist in armor warfare and came to the JSOA with no Special Forces experience. Senator William S. Cohen (R–Maine) has stated that "the Army . . . bypasssed all its special forces personnel and selected an armor officer to head the JSOA. The message seems to be clear—if you want to get ahead, don't serve in special forces."[77]

One of the chief obstacles to the establishment of an effective counterterrorism program stems from the Armed Services' de–emphasis of special operations following the conclusion of the Vietnam War. Coupled with the increased interest in general–purpose forces, a number of SOFs units were deactivated, with the subsequent loss of many highly trained, experienced and motivated officers and enlisted personnel. During the 1970s, and still today, Special Forces units were viewed as the backwaters of the Armed Services, ones to be avoided by those officers and enlisted personnel seeking successful careers. Thus the highest motivated officers and enlisted personnel sought assignment to units offering the best career tracks. In the words of former Deputy Assistant Secretary Koch, "there is a great disincentive to get involved in a sort of an activity which has no future, an enterprise which is not easily gold–plated, an enterprise in which you cannot step out of special operations into where you have a fat job with a defense contractor."[78] When the need for an effective response to terrorism became paramount at the end of the 1970s, the U.S. Special Forces consisted of dedicated officers and enlisted personnel. Yet these units were, and still are, staffed by personnel not representing the Armed Services' best and most experienced.[79] It will take time for the Reagan administration's efforts to strengthen SOFs to address this problem.

Another roadblock is the impact of the general–purpose force concept on the U.S. Army and its leadership. The general–purpose concept has been formulated to meet the conventional military problems created by expanding Soviet military capabilities. William J. Taylor, Jr., pointed out that "army leaders have insisted that forces able to survive in the NATO–Warsaw Pact war environment are capable of carrying out any mission in a less–intense environment."[80] This perception has reinforced a reluctance by the Armed Services to back Special Forces with the needed financial backing. Congressman Earl Hutto (D–Fla.), of the House's Special Operations Committee, has stated that "no one has said that we don't need special operations forces, but when it comes down to making a recommendation or budget proposal, well then the resources are not for special operations. They're asked for the conventional forces."[81] Despite the Armed Services' lack of interest in SOFs, both the Reagan administration and Congress have worked closely to increase the Special Forces budget from $441.0 million in 1982 to $1.2 billion in 1986.[82]

An illustration of the Armed Services' continuing lack of interest in SOFs is the Air Forces' failure to replace the helicopters lost during the Iranian hostage mission and its willingness, through Initiative 17, to turn over to the Army its special operations airlift functions. The Air Forces' actions has aroused concern within Congress that not enough is being done to address shortcomings in the Armed Services' handling of SOFs. In addition, the Air Forces' attitude and behavior are illustrative of former Deputy Assistant Secretary Koch's November 28, 1984, interview with Ted Koppel of ABC News Nightline. In response to Ted Koppel's question "Is not one of the problems, interservice rivalry, the fact that every particular branch of the service wants to have its own special operations?" Koch outlined the level of interest among the services for SOFs. He stated that "some of the services want their own operations forces," but "it's also true that a number of them want nothing to do with it, and some of them tried to divest themselves of any responsibility or capability whatsoever in the area of special operations."[83]

Ted Koppel's question to Deputy Assistant Secretary Koch also addresses the problem of service rivalry, which, as pointed out by Roger M. Pezzelle, are "indeed real."[84] The interservice, intraservice and intraunit conflicts over the development of Delta Force in the mid–1970s are illustrative of the impact of service rivalries and their obstacle to the establishment of an effective Defense Department response to terrorism. The formulation of Delta Force in November 1977 was viewed by those commanders of units with counterterrorist capabilities, like the Black Berets, as a threat to their unit's counterterrorist mission. A commander seeks to demonstrate his unit's importance by increasing its capabilities and mission responsibilities. Delta Force would, and did, undermine other units' importance by superseding one of their responsibilities. Delta Force was also viewed as a threat to other units' integrity. One of many obstacles Colonel Beckwith faced in constructing Delta Force was his inability to recruit personnel. Other commanders viewed Colonel Beckwith's attempts to recruit personnel from their units as an attack on their units' effectiveness. The loss of key personnel, such as NCOs and young officers, to Colonel Beckwith would undermine other units' combat capabilities.[85]

Another weakness with the DOD's response to terrorism is the general lack of understanding of the terrorist threat. Witness the conclusion of the Long

Commission report. This problem should be addressed by the implementation of an educational program designed to create a greater degree of awareness among officers, with the service academies beginning the process with a mandatory course on unconventional conflicts. A more comprehensive program beyond the academy level should be formulated to fit the requirements of each service. To increase awareness and understanding among civilian officials, the Defense Department in tandem with other departments should develop an educational program.

The controversy over the Air Forces' behavior toward SOFs and whether SOFs in general are being adequately funded has brought to the surface an internal power struggle in the spring of 1986, between the Defense Department's chief civilian officials concerned with SOFs, Deputy Assistant Secretary Koch and Assistant Secretary Latham. Koch, reportedly, was critical of recent department SOFs efforts and in late 1985 wrote a proposal addressing these problems. His proposal "painted a bleak picture of current SOF capabilities and planning." In addition, he was "reportedly maneuvering to control both the resources and policy aspects of the DOD's SOF oversight." Secretary Latham, reportedly, has defended the administration's party line that the department's revitalization of the SOF is moving ahead as planned.[86] This conflict was resolved with the resignation of Secretary Koch during the summer of 1986.

The conflict between Secretaries Koch and Lathem, the lack of political–military guidance and the finding by the House's Committee on Appropriations that "the command and control of Special Operations Force units is sufficiently ambiguous that there is an adverse impact on training and operations" illustrate the structural weaknesses of the DOD approach to unconventional threats and represent a major obstacle to the development of an effective response.[87] The major areas of weakness are associated with the nature of the Joint Chiefs of Staff and the division of Special Forces oversight duties within the Office of the Secretary of Defense. The Joint Chiefs of Staff, as outlined by William Lind of the Military Reform Institute, "is a system that is designed to produce lowest–common–denominator, committee–consensus solutions, which invariably are the worst approach to combat of any sort."[88] The current nature of the Joint Chiefs has undermined the development of the JSOA. The JSOA has not been able to develop the authority needed to influence special–operations affairs because of the lack of backing by the Joint Chiefs and their inability to create a powerful Director of the JSOA. One recommendation might be the elevating of the Director's position from a Major General to Lieutenant General level and giving the JSOA direct command over the JSOC.

Another possible solution might be to reconstitute the position of Special Assistant for Counterinsurgency and Special Activities (SACSA) to the Chairman of the Joint Chiefs of Staff. The SACSA should be considered the Armed Services' commander–in–chief for special–operation forces with responsibilities of controlling the U.S. counterterrorist military response, with command over the JSOC and the Office for Counterinsurgency and Special Activities (OCSA). The SACSA should hold the rank of Lieutenant General, with direct access to and control over any military asset required to execute an approved counterterrorism operation. He should also be supplied by the Joint Chiefs with enough authority to resolve any personal conflicts. The OCSA should assume the current functions of the JSOA and contain a staff of both military and civilian specialists in special operations. This proposal is compatible with recent Congressional efforts to strengthen the authority of the Chairman of the Joint Chiefs of Staff.

The current division of responsibilities for oversight of SOFs within the Office of the Secretary of Defense can best be corrected by the unification of these duties within one office. One unification proposal was the Senate's Committee on the Armed Services' recommendation of the creation of the Office of the Deputy Under Secretary for Low Intensity Warfare and Special Operations.[89] This proposal, however, was dropped from the committee's DOD reorganization bill. Another possible solution to the "sad state of affairs that [U.S.] SOF is in today" is the U.S. Armed Services' adoption of the structure and procedures used by one or more of the more successful special–operations forces, such as the British Special Air Services (SAS).[90] The original proposal for Delta Force, as offered by Colonel Beckwith, was patterned after the SAS. The SAS is one of the best if not the best special–operations forces in the world. Its reputation of overcoming obstacles and accomplishing difficult tasks, enhanced by its performances in the Falklands Islands War and the May 1980 rescue of hostages being held in the Iranian Embassy in London, has fostered a powerful and legendary mystique. An example of this mystique is offered by Tony Geraghty, a freelance author and journalist. He stated that "in December 1975, a Provisional IRA team, trapped in a flat at Balcombe Street, Marylebone, with a middle–age couple living there as hostages, surrendered to the London police when the BBC announced that the SAS was on the scene, ready to attack."[91] A report to the U.S. House of Representatives' Committee on Appropriations entitled the "Special Operations Forces of the Department of Defense" issued by the Subcommittee on the Defense Department's Surveys and Investigations Staff during February 1986 stated that the SAS's success extends from its being "considered a national asset and is so–funded; there is unity of command; its forces are tasked at the highest level and only for the most important operations; and once tasked and committed, the commander in the field has total operational control."[92] However, due to the reasons outlined earlier, it is doubtful that the U.S. military would accept the SAS or any other foreign unit as a model for its special–operations force.

By the late summer of 1985 a growing sense of frustration over the lack of progress in improving United States SOF had led a number of supporters of reform to express concern and doubts about the DOD's ability to improve its special–operation forces. Supporting the need for change, Congressman Dan Daniel (D-Va.), chairman of the House's Armed Services Committee's Readiness Subcommittee, stated that the alternatives of either establishing a Defense Agency for Special Operations or a unified command or transferring all SOF elements to a single military service "would go a long way toward" enhancing the U.S. response to unconventional threats.[93] The growing sense of frustration over the lack of SOF reform ultimately led to the resignation of Deputy Assistant Secretary of Defense for ISA Noel C. Koch in the summer of 1986.

Responding to the continuing intransigeance on the part of the DOD to provide the "big fix" seen by many supporters of SOF reform as the only solution to the problems affecting special–operations, Congress on October 15, 1986 approved and President Reagan signed into law on November 14, 1986 the "Fiscal Year 1987 National Defense Authorization Bill." Attached to this bill was a provision by Senator William S. Cohen (R-Maine) mandating the establishment of an Assistant Secretary of Defense for Special Operations and Low–Intensity Conflict and a unified SOF command.[94] Congress' action is seen, as outlined by Michael Ganley, a contributing editor to *Armed Forces Journal International*, as reflecting "the view that the organizational arrangement for Special Operations Forces should be institutionalized to provide long–term stability."[95] However, as of February 1987 the exact duties of the new Assistant Secretary for Special Operations and Low–Intensity Conflict had not been outlined.[96] Yet, for the new position to be an effective and strong advocate for special operations it must assume the special operations and counterterrorism policy duties of the Office of the Assistant Secretary of Defense for International Security Affairs and the budget and oversight responsibilities currently executed by the Assistant Secretary of Defense for Command, Control, Communications and Intelligence.

The exact duties, responsibilities, location and commander of the new unified SOF command, like the new Assistant Secretary, as of February 1987 had not been outlined. The new commander, as outlined by the Cohen provision, should be either a full general or admiral and be "responsible for SOF training, doctrine, strategy, tactics, combat readiness, and establishing priorities for requirements."[97] A unified command, as outlined by John M. Collins, Senior Specialist in National Defense, Library of Congress, is "a top-echelon U.S. combatant organization with regional or functional responsibilities, which normally is comprised of forces from two or more Military Services."[98] It is hoped that the new unified SOF command, once fully operational, will assume the policy and planning functions of the Joint Special Operations Agency and command over the Joint Special Operations Command and its units. The reforms mandated by the Cohen provision represent the type of bold steps needed to correct the problems affecting the Armed Services' special forces efforts, because for the U.S. policy toward international terrorism to have any credence, America must develop and implement an effective military capability. This capability should be part of a recognition by both civilian and military leaders that the most likely types of conflict through the rest of the 1980s and into the 1990s will be unconventional and will take place in those regions of the world in which U.S. interest and influence have traditionally been limited.

NOTES

1.   U.S. Department of State, *Realism, Strength, Negotiations: Key Foreign Policy Statements of the Reagan Administration* (Washington, D.C.: U.S. Department of State, Bureau of Public Affairs, May 1984), p. 8.

2.   "Secret Policy on Terrorism Given Airing," *The Washington Post*, 18 April 1984, p. A1.

3.   "Preemptive Anti-Terrorist Raids Allowed," *The Washington Post*, 16 April 1984, p. A19.

4.   Ibid.

5.   "Secret Policy on Terrorism Given Airing," p. A1.

6.   "Terrorism and Hypocrisy," *The Washington Post*, 7 November 1984, p. A16.

7.   "U.S. Learning How to React if Terror Threatens," *The New York Times*, 2 December 1984, p. A16; ABC, "This Week with David Brinkley," 12 January 1986, Show #220, David Brinkley, moderator, p. 2.

8.   *Report of the Secretary of State's Advisory Panel on Overseas Security*, Admiral Bobby Inman, USN (Ret.), chairman (Washington, D.C.: Department of State, June 1985), p. 47.

9.   U.S. Congress, House, Subcommittee on the Department of Defense of the Committee on Appropriations, *Department of Defense Appropriations for 1987: Special Operations Forces*, 99th Cong., 2d sess., 10 April 1986, p. 534.

10.   U.S. Congress, House, Subcommittee on the Department of Defense of the Committee on Appropriations, *Department of Defense Appropriations for 1986: Special Operations Forces*, 99th Cong., 1st sess., 7 May 1985, p. 607.

11.   Shelby L. Stanton, *Green Berets at War* (Novato, Calif.: Presidio Press, 1985), p. 51.

12. U.S. Congress, House, Subcommittee on the Department of Defense of the Committee on Appropriations, *Department of Defense Appropriations for 1987: Special Operations Forces*, p. 624.

13. Deborah G. Meyer and Benjamin F. Schemmer, "An Exclusive AFJ Interview with: Noel C. Koch, Principal Deputy Assistant Secretary of Defense for International Security Affairs," *Armed Forces Journal International* (March 1985): 36.

14. U.S. Congress, Senate, Committee on Governmental Affairs, *An Act to Combat International Terrorism: Hearings on S. 2236*, 95th Cong., 2d sess., 22 February 1978, p. 191.

15. U.S. Congress, House, Subcommittee on the Department of Defense of the Committee on Appropriations, *Department of Defense Appropriations for 1985: Special Operations Forces*, 98th Cong., 2d sess., 10 April 1984, p. 834.

16. Ibid.

17. Telephone conversation with Lieutenant Colonel McHugh, Terrorism Section, U.S. Army Department of Defense (695–4133), October 7, 1983.

18. U.S. Congress, Senate, Committee on Governmental Affairs, *An Act to Combat International Terrorism: Hearings on S. 2236*, 22 February 1978, p. 192.

19. Richard H. Shultz, Jr., "The State of the Operational Art: A Critical Review of Anti-terrorist Programs," in *Responding to the Terrorist Threat: Security and Crisis Management*, ed., Richard H. Shultz, Jr., and Stephen Sloan (New York: Pergamon Press, 1980), p. 33.

20. Ibid.

21. Henry Kissinger, *White House Years* (Boston: Little, Brown and Company, 1979), p. 658.

22. Benjamin F. Schemmer, *The Raid* (New York: Harper & Row Publishers, 1976), pp. 49–50.

23. Shultz, "The State of the Operational Art," p. 34.

24. Neil C. Livingstone, *The War against Terrorism* (Lexington, Mass.: Lexington Books, 1982), p. 187.

25. U.S. Congress, Senate, Committee on Governmental Affairs, *An Act to Combat International Terrorism: Hearings on S. 2236*, 22 February 1978, pp. 195–197.

26. Lt. Col. Tom Hamrick, U.S. Army (Ret.), "The Black Berets," *Army* (May 1977): 29.

27. Livingstone, *War against Terrorism*, pp. 177–178.

28. Col. Charlie A. Beckwith, USA (Ret.), and Donald Knox, *Delta Force* (New York: Harcourt Brace Jovanovich, 1983), p. 133.

29. Ibid., p. 122.

30. Ibid., p. 119.

31. Ibid., p. 166.

32. Gary Sick, "Military Options and Constraints," in *American Hostages in Iran: The Conduct of a Crisis*, by Warren Christopher et. al. (New Haven: Yale University Press, 1985), p. 144.

33. William J. Taylor, Jr., and Steven A. Maaranen, eds., *The Future of Conflict in the 1980s* (Lexington, Mass.: Lexington Books, 1982), p. 470.

34. Robert W. Komer, "How to Prepare for Low-Intensity Conflict in the 1980s," in *The Future of Conflict in the 1980s*, ed. William J. Taylor, Jr., and Steven A. Maaranen (Lexington, Mass.: Lexington Books, 1982), p. 23.

35. Michael C. Ryan, "Combat Rescue Operations," in *The Future of Conflict in the 1980s*, ed. William J. Taylor, Jr., and Steven A. Maaranen (Lexington, Mass.: Lexington Books, 1982), p. 196.

36. Beckwith and Knox, *Delta Force*, pp. 299–300.

37. Ibid.

38. Paul B. Ryan, *The Iranian Rescue Mission: Why It Failed* (Annapolis, Md.: Naval Institute Press, 1985), p. 109.

39. Ibid., p. 123.

40. U.S. Congress, House, Subcommittee on the Department of Defense of the Committee on Appropriations, *Department of Defense Appropriations for 1985: Special Operations Forces*, p. 835.

41. John O. Marsh, Jr., "Keynote Address," in *Special Operations in U.S. Strategy*, ed. Frank R. Barnett, B. Hugh Tovar, and Richard H. Shultz (Washington, D.C.: National Defense University Press, 1984), p. 18.

42. Ibid., p. 19.

43. John F. Murphy, "Report on Conference on International Terrorism: Protection of Diplomatic Premises and Personnel, Bellagio, Italy, March 8–12, 1982," *Terrorism: An International Journal* 6, no. 3 (1983): 485.

44. Ibid.

45. U.S. Congress, House, Subcommittee on Readiness of the Committee on Armed Services, *Special Operations Forces*, 98th Cong., 2d sess., 2 March 1983, p. 17.

46. Ibid., pp. 17–18.

47. Meyer and Schemmer, "An Exclusive AFJ Interview," p. 48.

48. Report, William S. Lind, Military Reform Institute, to the Congressional Military Reform Caucus, April 5, 1984, p. 2.

49. Richard A. Gabriel, *Military Incompetence: Why the American Military Doesn't Win* (New York: Hill and Wang, 1985), p. 161.

50. Colonel Harry G. Summers, Jr., U.S. Army, "Delta Force: America's Counterterrorist Unit and the Mission to Rescue the Hostages in Iran," *Military Review* (November 1983): 21–27 passim.

51. U.S. Congress, Senate, *Congressional Record*, 98th Cong., 2d sess., 1984: S359.

52. Ibid., p. S361.

53. U.S. Congress, House, Subcommittee on the Department of Defense of the Committee on Appropriations, *Department of Defense Appropriations for 1985: Special Operations Forces*, pp. 797–798.

54. Ibid., p. 789.

55. Ibid., p. 806.

56. Ibid., p. 799.

57. Ibid., pp. 799–800

58. Ibid., p. 800.

59. "U.S. Military Tries to Catch Up in Fighting Terror," *The New York Times*, 5 December 1984, p. A8.

60. U.S. Congress, Senate *Congressional Record*, p. S359.

61. R. William Mengel, "The Impact of Nuclear Terrorism on the Military's Role in Society," in *International Terrorism in the Contemporary World*, ed. Marius H. Livingston et al. (Westport, Conn.: Greenwood Press, 1978), pp. 411–412.

62. Schlomo Gazit and Michael Handel, "Insurgency, Terrorism and Intelligence," in *Intelligence Requirements for the 1980s: Counter-Intelligence*, ed. Roy Godson (Washington, D.C.: National Strategy Information Center, 1980), p. 141.

63. William J.Taylor, Jr., "Psychological Operations in the Spectrum of Conflict in the 1980s," in *The Future of Conflict in the 1980s*, ed. William J. Taylor, Jr., and Steve A. Maaranen (Lexington, Mass.: Lexington Books, 1982), p. 123.

64. Ibid., p. 114.

65. U.S. Congress, House, Subcommittee on the Department of Defense of the Committee on Appropriations, *Department of Defense Appropriations for 1985: Special Operations Forces*, p. 800.

66. Ibid., p. 827.

67. U.S. Armed Services, *Joint Special Operations Agency (JSOA), Joint Manpower Program (JMP)—FY 1984: Approved*, 25 June 1984, p. 23.

68. U.S. Congress, House, Subcommittee on the Department of Defense of the Committee on Appropriations, *Department of Defense Appropriations for 1986: Special Operations Forces*, pp. 603–604.

69. Noel C. Koch, "Two Cases against a Sixth Service," *Armed Forces Journal International* (October 1985): 109.

70. Dr. Edward N. Luttwak, "Discussion" of Roger M. Pezzelle, "Military Capabilities and Special Operations in the 1980s," in *Special Operations in U.S. Strategy*, ed. Frank R. Barnett, B. Hugh Tovar, and Richard H. Shultz (Washington, D.C.: National Defense University Press, 1984), p. 155.

71. Deborah G. Meyer, "Four Years Later: Desert One Revisited?" *Armed Forces Journal International* (August 1985): 26.

72. U.S. Department of State, *Counterterrorism Policy*, Bureau of Public Affairs' Circular no. 823 (Washington, D.C.: U.S. Department of State, Bureau of Public Affairs, Office of Communications, April 1986), p. 1.

73. Maurice Tugwell and David Charters, "Special Operations and the Threats to United States Interests in the 1980s," in *Special Operations in U.S. Strategy*, ed. Frank R. Barnett, B. Hugh Tovar, and Richard H. Shultz (Washington, D.C.: National Defense University Press, 1984), p. 35.

74. William V. O'Brien, "Special Operations in the 1980s: American Moral, Legal, Political, and Cultural Constraints," in *Special Operations in U.S. Strategy*, ed. Frank R. Barnett, B. Hugh Tovar, and Richard H. Shultz (Washington, D.C.: National Defense University Press, 1984), p. 71.

75. Stanton, *Green Berets*, p. 3.

76. Roger M. Pezzelle, "Military Capabilities and Special Operations in the 1980s," in *Special Operations in U.S. Strategy*, ed. Frank R. Barnett, B. Hugh Tovar, and Richard H. Shultz (Washington, D.C.: National Defense University Press, 1984), p. 147–148.

77. Michael Ganley, "New Unified Command for Special Ops Proposed by Senators Cohen and Nunn," *Armed Forces Journal International* (June 1986): 18.

78. ABC News, "Nightline," 28 November 1984, show #918, Ted Koppel, moderator, p. 2.

79. Charles M. Simpson III, *Inside the Green Berets: The First Thirty Years* (Novanto, Calif.: Presidio Press, 1983), pp. 215–222 passim.

80. William J. Taylor, Jr., "Future Trends and Phenomena: Impact on the Army," in *Strategic Requirements for the Army to the Year 2000*, ed. Robert H. Kupperman and William J. Taylor, Jr. (Lexington, Mass.: Lexington Books, 1984), p. 60.

81. ABC News, "Nightline," 28 November 1984, p. 3.

82. "A Warrior Elite for the Dirty Jobs," *Time*, January 13, 1986, p. 16.

83. ABC News, "Nightline, 28 November 1984, p. 4.

84. Pezzelle, "Military Capabilities," p. 151.

85. Beckwith and Knox, *Delta Force*, passim.

86. Deborah G. Meyer and Benjamin F. Schemmer, Congressional Pressure May Force Far More DOD Dollars for Special Ops, *Armed Forces Journal International* (April 1986): 22.

87. U.S. Congress, House, Committee on Appropriations, *Department of Defense Appropriation Bill, 1986: Report to Accompany H.R. 3629*, 99th Cong., 1st sess., 1985, H. Rept. 332, p. 43.

88. ABC News, "Nightline," 28 November 1984, p. 2.

89. U.S. Congress, Senate, Committee on Armed Services, *Defense Organization: The Need for Change: Staff Report*, 99th Cong., 1st sess., 1985, S. Prt. 86, p. 102.

90. Charles D. Odorizzi, "SOF Reorganization: Everyone Has a Plan—Senate, House, and DOD," *Armed Forces Journal International* (September 1986): 17.

91. Tony Geraghty, *This Is the SAS: A Pictorial History of the Special Air Service Regiment* (London: Arms and Armour Press, 1982), p. 86.

92. U.S. Congress, House, Subcommittee on the Department of Defense of the Committee on Appropriations, *Department of Defense Appropriations for 1987: Special Operations Forces*, p. 557.

93. Rep. Dan Daniel (D–Va.), "U.S. Special Operations: The Case for a Sixth Service," *Armed Forces Journal International* (August 1985): 74.

94. Michael Ganley, "Congress Creates New Unified Command for SOF and New Civilian SOF Chief," *Armed Forces Journal International* (November 1986): 20.

95. Ibid.

96. Charles D. Odorizzi: and Benjamin F. Schemmer, "JCS and OSD Torn on Organizing New Special Operations Hierarchies," *Armed Forces Journal International* (February 1987): 49.

97. Ganley, "Congress Creates New Unified Command for SOF," p. 20.

98. John M. Collins, *U.S. Defense Planning: A Critique* (Boulder, Colo.: Westview Press, 1982), p. 313.

6

The Intelligence Community
and Terrorism

The most important aspect of any nation's fight against domestic and international terrorism is current and accurate intelligence. Robert H. Kupperman, Executive Director of Georgetown University's Center for Strategic and International Studies, stated that "intelligence is the first line of defense."[1] "Sound, up-to-date intelligence," as outlined by former Director of the Department of State's Office for Combatting Terrorism, Ambassador Anthony Quainton, "is essential if we are to be informed in advance of likely incidents. Without it we cannot take the necessary counter-measures nor will we have available sufficient information on which to make decisions in an actual crisis situation."[2]

President Reagan's signing of National Security Decision Directive (NSDD) 138 signaled a rechanneling and repositioning of U.S. intelligence resources and posture toward combatting terrorism. The U.S. traditional intelligence strategy toward terrorism from the late 1960s to 1984 was defensive and passive. This strategy was, and still is, designed, as pointed out by Schlomo Gazit, former Director, Israel Military Intelligence, and Michael Handel, a member of Harvard University's Center for International Affairs, "to give a warning on the appearance of an underground terrorist threat even before it has started to operate."[3] However, NSDD 138, "a 'decision in principle' to use force against terrorism," calls for an active counterstrategy.[4] An active counterstrategy, as outlined by Gazit and Handel, is composed of four components. The first component is comprised of actions executed by a nation within its own borders to deny a terrorist group the needed material, structural and psychological support. Next, the counterstrategy is comprised of covert and/or overt actions carried out outside a nation's own border for the purpose of bringing pressure on other governments supporting terrorism in order to force them away from supporting terrorism or giving terrorists sanctuary. Finally, the active counterstrategy is pictured as consisting of "a variety of deception and disinformation operations" and "operations intended to create intrigues, friction, and intraorganizational conflicts or conflicts between terrorist organizations."[5]

The intelligence community presently consists of ten departments and agencies.[6] Among them, the Central Intelligence Agency (CIA), the Federal Bureau of Investigation (FBI), the Department of State's Bureau of Intelligence and Research, the Defense Intelligence Agency, the National Security Agency and the intelligence units of the Armed Services have a direct role in dealing with terrorism.[7] During the Carter administration, executive order 12036 defined the intelligence community's role in dealing with terrorism as one designed to "coordinate the collection, analysis and dissemination of covert information and intelligence on terrorists and their potential targets.[8] On December 4, 1981, President Reagan signed executive order 12333, which revoked executive order 12036 and altered the functions of the intelligence community.[9] The executive order's purpose is "to enhance human and technical collection techniques, especially those undertaken abroad, and the acquisition of significant foreign intelligence, as well as the detection and countering of international terrorist activities."[10] In dealing with terrorism specifically, the order describes the intelligence community's role as the "collection of information concerning, and the conduct of activities to protect against international terrorism . . . and other hostile activities directed against the United States by foreign powers, organizations, persons and their agents."[11]

The intelligence community's resources and assets in executing its responsibilities can be divided into two areas: collection resources and operational assets.[12] No matter what intelligence strategy is used in combatting terrorism, the collection, analysis and dissemination of covert and overt information are vital to the success of U.S. anti- and counterterrorist efforts. The CIA, the Bureau of Intelligence and Research and the FBI are the chief intelligence collection agencies. The CIA, through the use of a computer known as Octopus, assembles all available data on the movements and activities of known and suspected terrorists.[13] Octopus represents the backbone of U.S. physical security programs, such as the Lookout System.

The FBI, through its Terrorist Research and Analytical Center, annually produces unclassified data on terrorist activities, mainly domestic terrorist trends. The Bureau of Intelligence and Research of the State Department produces and disseminates current information that relates directly to the department's own broad and complex antiterrorist program and to that of the American overall response. During the Carter administration, the State Department's Office for Combatting Terrorism reviewed and disseminated all intelligence material relating to terrorism. Through the mid–1980s the State Department's Office for Counter–terrorism and Emergency Planning and then its successor, the Office of the Ambassador–at–Large for Counterterrorism, handled this task.[14] In addition, during the late 1970s, in order to improve further the intelligence community's efforts, a special committee existed "to focus on the important tasks of coordinating intelligence flow and improve overall terrorist intelligence coverage."[15] It was also assigned "special intelligence problems and concerns referred to it by the National Security Council/Special Coordination Committee's Working Group on Terrorism."[16] Unfortunately, due to the Reagan administration's tightening of the flow of information concerning the U.S. response to terrorism, it can only be assumed that a special committee similar to the Carter administration's exists. However, if such a committee exists, it is most likely a component of the National Security Council's (NSC's) Senior Interagency Group for Intelligence, chaired by the Director of Central Intelligence. As outlined by a January 12, 1982, statement by the President entitled "National Security Council Structure," the Senior Interagency Group for Intelligence is required to "submit to the NSC an overall annual assessment of the relative threat to United States interests from intelligence and security services of foreign powers and from international terrorist activities including an assessment of the effectiveness of the United States counterintelligence activities."[17] Finally, in a move to improve coordination within the intelligence community, several intelligence units, such as the State Department's Bureau of Research and Intelligence, have established 24–hour watches on international terrorism.[18]

The intelligence community's chief operational functions are counterintelligence operations and special activities (covert actions). Executive order 12333 defines *counterintelligence* as "information gathered and activities conducted to protect against espionage, other intelligence activities, sabotage, or assassinations conducted for or on behalf of foreign powers, organizations or persons, or international terrorist activities, but not including personnel, physical, document or communications security programs."[19] Presently, six organizational units of the intelligence community are authorized to conduct counterintelligence functions outside and within the United States: the CIA, the FBI and the intelligence elements of the Army, Navy, Air Force and Marine Corps. Currently, all counterintelligence operations occurring outside the United States are coordinated by the Central Intelligence Agency. All counterintelligence activities taking place within the United States are coordinated by the FBI and are executed in accordance with the Attorney General's Guidelines for Domestic Security Investigations ("Levi Guidelines").[20]

The intelligence community's second operational function consists of *special activities* (covert actions) that executive order 12333 defines as:

> activities conducted in support of national foreign policy objectives abroad which are planned and executed so that the role of the United States Government is not apparent or acknowledged publicly, and functions in support activities, but which are not intended to influence United States political processes, public opinion, policies, or media and do not include diplomatic activities or the collection and production of intelligence or related support functions.[21]

Neither executive order 1233 nor NSDD 138 permits assassinations.[22] Only the CIA under the approval of the President is authorized to execute special activities. The CIA's authority to fulfill the President's and the NSC's special foreign policy requests extends from the National Security Act of 1947. Yet its capabilities in executing special activities were not formulated until June 18, 1948, with the NSC's approval of NSC 10/2, which established the Office of Special Projects. The office was directed "to plan and conduct covert operations."[23] The Office of Special Projects has evolved into the present Directorate of Operations, which represents the intelligence community's chief operational asset in combatting international terrorism.

The CIA forms the backbone of U.S. anti– and counterterrorism intelligence efforts. However, the details surrounding the nature of U.S. counterintelligence and special activities are classified. This excludes the possibility of any type of in–depth examination of their utility in combatting terrorism. However, on August 16, 1978, while appearing before the House of Representatives' Subcommittee on Civil and Constitutional Rights, Ambassador Quainton as Chairman of the Working Group on Terrorism stated that in the areas of collecting, analyzing and disseminating information on terrorism, "I have been satisfied that we are getting adequate support from members of the intelligence community."[24] More recently, Ambassador Robert B. Oakley, the State Department's Ambassador–at–Large for Counterterrorism (designate), on June 16, 1986, in an address before the U.S. Conference of Mayors in San Juan, Puerto Rico, cited improved intelligence collection as helping to "deter or preempt more than 180 international terrorist actions over the past 18 months."[25] However, a number of individuals would disagree with the Ambassador's remarks and have severely questioned the capabilities of the intelligence community in combatting terrorism. Abram Shulsky, a professional staff member of the Senate Intelligence Committee, has stated that the U.S. intelligence community lacks the capabilities to implement either a defensive-passive strategy or an active counterstrategy in dealing with terrorism.[26] In addition, a report by the Surveys and Investigations staff entitled "Special Operations Forces of the Department of Defense" issued in February 1986 for the U.S. House of Representatives' Committee on Appropriations states flatly that "there is a lack of timely and sufficient intelligence support for special operations forces."[27] Finally, the continued incarceration of a number of Americans in Lebanon by unknown terrorists demonstrates a lack of capabilities on the part of the intelligence community that is shocking and frustrating, given President Reagan's May 31, 1986, statement that: "History may well record that 1986 was the year when the world came to grips with the plague of international terrorism."[28] The intelligence community's inability or desire to identify the terrorists and/or take appropriate, given the duration of these hostage episodes, undermines the credibility of U.S. anti- and counterterrorist actions. The rescue of these Americans would demonstrate a counterterrorist capability on the part of the U.S. intelligence community that would have a much greater impact on the prevention, deterrence and suppression of terrorism directed toward Americans than any type of retaliatory strike or raid. No matter how discriminate a retaliatory action is, innocent individuals are always hurt. In combatting terrorism, a nation should seek to punish only those responsible and not engage in some type of indiscriminate violence carried out by terrorists. The rescue of the hostages would demonstrate a U.S. ability to do just that.

Whether or not the intelligence community lacks the capabilities to deal effectively with terrorism, it still is confronted with a number of obstacles in its fight against terrorism. The first is the nature of terrorist groups. They are small and homogeneous and are comprised of individuals that are closely related by family or friendship. As pointed out by Brian Jenkins of the Rand Corporation, "they are seldom sophisticated enough to be vulnerable to sophisticated intelligence-gathering techniques, such as electronic surveillance."[29] The main source of intelligence about terrorist groups is gathered by human intelligence means. However, because of the nature of terrorist groups, they are difficult to penetrate.[30]

Unfortunately, as outlined by the Long Commission Report, U.S. human-intelligence capabilities are inadequate. On December 19, 1983, the House of Representatives' Investigative Subcommittee of the Committee on the Armed Services issued a summary of its findings and conclusions concerning the U.S. Maine Corps' security arrangements in Beirut and, in the area of intelligence support, stated that the "Marine Amphibious Unit (MAU) in Lebanon did not receive adequate intelligence support dealing with terrorism. Serious intelligence inadequacies had a direct effect on the capability of the unit to defend itself against the full spectrum of threat."[31]

American human-intelligence capabilities have been greatly affected by past abuses of the functions of the intelligence community, by Congressional examinations of these abuses and by past deemphasis of human-intelligence techniques. The Reagan administration has attempted to increase the intelligence community's capabilities by enhancing funding and loosening of constraints on its ability to carry out counterintelligence and special activities. However, the administration's loosening of constraints on the intelligence community to conduct certain types of operations could rekindle a strong backlash by the American public and Congress, as demonstrated by their reaction to the Iran arms-for-hostages affair. Past abuses in this area and response by Congress led, in the 1970s, to the formulation of a number of legislative acts, which have been cited as constraints on the intelligence community's ability to deal with terrorism. Allegedly, the most harmful legislative measure has been the Freedom of Information Act of 1974. As pointed out by Ambassador Quainton, "the opening of government files under Freedom of Information procedures has had the unexpected consequence of retricting the flow of information between governments."[32] U.S. allies have expressed concern that the provisions of the Freedom of Information Act would lead to the public disclosure of sensitive intelligence and expose key sources of information and thus has, reportedly, produced a restricted exchange of information on terrorism.

Although concern has been expressed, there is no evidence to support the fears associated with the Freedom of Information Act. Additionally, Congress in 1984, in a move to protect sensitive intelligence "sources and methods," amended the Freedom of Information Act. Unfortunately, concern over possible misuse or abuse of the intelligence community as been rekindled by the Reagan administration's disinformation program directed against Colonel Khaddafi. The goal for this action was to "combine real and illusionary events—through a disinformation program—[so as to make] Khaddafi think that there was a high degree of internal opposition to him within Libya, that his key trusted aides were disloyal and that the U.S. was about to move against him militarily."[33] The goal of keeping the Khaddafi regime off balance is one thing, but when a nation's leadership makes a conscious effort, as in this case, of lying to the public, it damages the trust and credibility that is vital to the health of any democracy. Nothing is more valuable than the protection of those institutions and values that the United States has traditionally stood for. The Reagan administration's disinformation program is an illustration of its lack of understanding of terrorism and leads one to conclude that perhaps it has lost sight of what are the real threats to the United States. Further contributing to the perception that the Reagan administration has failed to understand the terrorism issue and to concern on the part of Congress that the intelligence community is being misused is the Iran arms-for-hostages affair. Many of the adverse aspects of this affair and how they have affected U.S. policy toward terrorism have already been outlined. However, it is still disappointing that the Reagan administration would consciously deal with the same government that held hostage U.S. officials for 444 days and had a hand in the murder of 241 U.S. Marines and at the same time knowingly violated U.S. law in not informing both the Senate's and House's intelligence oversight committees. The Reagan administration's behavior demonstrated a lack of respect for the role of the Congress's intelligence committees specifically and in general the entire governmental process.

The Reagan administration's attempt to increase the intelligence community's capabilities in dealing with terrorism have been criticized for lack of specifics. An example is Section 2.3(a) of executive order 12333. This section states that the intelligence community is authorized to collect, retain and disseminate information on Americans during an international terrorism investigation. However, no definition of *international terrorism* is incorporated into the order.[34] This raises an important question concerning the authority of the intelligence community to investigate Americans and possible violations of American's civil liberties. Terrorist behavior, depending on the perception of an individual, can range from orderly street demonstrations to hijackings and assassinations. The provisions of executive order 12333 thus authorize the investigation of any American who engages in behavior that the U.S. government is suspicious of. Orders such as executive order 12333 must be specific in their use of terms like *terrorism*. In addition, to avoid abuses of the past, oversight by the intelligence committees of Congress is vital for both the protection of American civil liberties and the integrity of the intelligence community.

Another obstacle confronting the intelligence community in dealing with terrorism is the lack of continuity and permanence among top officials of the CIA's Directorate of Operations during this present administration. An example is the June 30, 1984, transfer of the following officials: John Stein, Director of Clandestine Operations; Charles Briggs, Executive Director of the CIA; Clair George, head of Legislative Liaison; James Taylor, Inspector General. The four officials exchanged positions with John Stein becoming Inspector General, Clair George becoming Director of Clandestine Operations, Charles Briggs becoming the agency's chief Congressional liaison and James Taylor becoming the agency's Executive Director.[35]

A further obstacle confronting the intelligence community, one closely associated with the lack of stability among the CIA's leadership, is the adverse effects of bureaucratic pressures and lack of leadership on the coordination and dissemination of intelligence. Wayne A. Kerstetter, a member of the American Society of International Law (ASIL) study of terrorism of the mid-1970s, has stated that although the National Security Council has improved the coordination capacity of the United States to deal with terrorism, the centralization of the collection process for intelligence has not been taken. This failure, according to Kerstetter, to centralize the process because of the lack of strong leadership has led to the duplication of effort and poor intergovernment working relationships.[36] Echoing Kerstetter concerns, Senator Jeremiah Denton (R-Ala.), Chairman of the Senate's Subcommittee on Security and Terrorism of the Judiciary Committee, in the spring of 1985, stated:

> There appears to be a great need to coordinate the collection and analysis of the information we get. We have the FBI, Department of State, CIA, the Defense Intelligence Agency, NSA, DEA, and various Armed Forces Intelligence groups collecting, analyzing, and disseminating information of terrorism. And, although there is some measure of coordination and cooperation, it is not sufficient. We must ensure adequate and appropriate efforts among all our agencies in every step of the intelligence process.[37]

To enhance the collection, dissemination and analysis of intelligence relating to terrorism, an intelligence review group should be established under the direction of the proposed Deputy National Security Adviser for Low-Intensity Conflicts. The review group should be divided into two staffs. The first should be responsible for policy formulation and coordination, and consist of officials from the chief antiterrorist intelligence units and the chief antiterrorist officials of the Departments of Defense and State and other major agencies. This staff should meet only at times of need or only every three or four months, and its operations should be closely coordinated with overall U.S. foreign policy and intelligence goals. The second staff should be an intelligence review staff that functions around the clock, with a staff consisting of officials from offices such as the State Department's Office of the Ambassador-at-Large for Counterterrorism and from the NSC. Its responsibility should be that of an intelligence central clearinghouse, designed to disseminate incoming intelligence quickly and accurately as possible to the appropriate agencies.

Finally, the politicization of the intelligence community has raised questions concerning its ability to objectively collect, analyze and disseminate information on terrorism. The Reagan administration has placed a high priority on information concerning international terrorism. During the first days of the Reagan administration, Secretary of State Haig and other top officials in and out of the administration sought to link Soviet behavior with that of international terrorism. The intelligence community, however, could not produce evidence to support the statements of Secretary Haig and others and still cannot. While on the issue of terrorism, there is no direct evidence that politicalization is harming the intelligence community's functions. However, the resignation of John R. Horton, formerly a senior analyst on Latin America for the CIA and National Intelligence Council, still keeps alive the fears that the present administration's ideological considerations are affecting the functions of the intelligence community. John Horton resigned in May 1984 over Director of Central Intelligence William Casey's rewriting of "an intelligence evaluation on Mexico over Horton's objections."[38] To combat terrorism effectively the U.S. response must not be colored by an administration's political or ideological considerations. The American response must be objective and bipartisan.

The obstacles confronting the intelligence community in combatting terrorism are very difficult issues not open to simple solutions. Any attempt to resolve these issues must deal with the problem of the proper balance between national security interests and the protection of civil liberties. However, no matter which solutions are implemented to enhance the intelligence community's capabilities, questions exist concerning its ability to produce good intelligence. Ambassador Anthony Quainton has stated: "Intelligence is the first and in some ways the critical element in combatting terrorism. It is not only a means of forewarning but also a necessary adjunct of response. . . . But good intelligence will never be available in adequate depth, and no law enforcement agency can rely on it to the exclusion of other methods."[39]

The Reagan administration's tough antiterrorist posture, represented by NSDD 138, raises a series of key foreign policy questions. The first is concerned with the legality of using self-help measures in combatting international terrorism. As stated by John F. Murphy, a member of the ASIL's mid-1970s study on terrorism, the use and implementation of "economic sanctions, the bringing of international claims, diplomatic protests, and quiet diplomacy are all permissible measures of state self-help under public international law against states supporting international terrorism."[40] The primary international legal concern is over the use of coercive measures or force in dealing with terrorism and its supporters. This question is examined in the next chapter.

The second question is associated with the possible economic consequences of an aggressive response to terrorism and its supporters. A number of Middle Eastern regimes, like Iran, Libya and Syria, are some of the most active supporters of international terrorism. The United States has cut its economic ties with those states accused of supporting international terrorism, such as Libya. Yet American European allies, such as Italy, still maintain strong economic relations with Libya and other states. If the United States were to attempt to remove one of these regimes through the use of special activities or by other means, it would risk the possibility of disturbing that state's economy, mainly oil production, to the point of harming the European economies and thus the United States. As a result of the interdependence of the present international economic order, any attempt by the United States to use self-help measures, like economic sanctions and reprisals, must deal with possible economic consequences.

On April 3, 1984, Secretary of State Shultz raised another important question concerning NSDD 138's utility by accusing Iran, Syria, Libya and North Korea of supporting international terrorism. A number of regimes accused of supporting international terrorism are Soviet friends or allies. An attempt by the United States to destroy subversive centers located in these nations risks a conflict with the Soviet Union. Such a possibility outweighs any benefit from the destruction of a terrorist training center. In addition, the Soviets' commitment to its allies, such as Syria, and not toward Libya helps explain to a degree the Reagan administration's aggressive behavior toward Colonel Khaddafi and reserved attitude toward Syria.

Another set of issues raised by NSDD 138 is concerned with the political consequences of using force. Pariah states such as South Africa and Israel have carried out reprisal raids against suspected terrorist bases. However, as pointed out by Ernest Evans, a Research Associate with the Brookings Institution, a major problem associated with a policy that uses reprisals is that it "aggravates the relations of the state undertaking the reprisal with normally friendly states."[41] South Africa and other such states can afford to aggravate relations with other states and ignore international condemnation of their actions. The United States, on the other hand, cannot afford to aggravate state relations and ignore international response. The goal of U.S. foreign policy is a stable international order, based on accepted norms of conduct. However, this goal is undermined by unilateral state actions that violate these norms and ignore international response and opinion. Unilateral state actions like reprisal raids promote an unstable anarchical world order.

President Reagan and other top administration officials have consistently pronounced a policy of swift and effective retribution in combatting international terrorism. This type of statement is representative of the administration's aggressive foreign policy style and raises doubts about its proper application and effectiveness in combatting terrorism. In responding to terrorism, the United States should recognize that no matter how rigorously pursued, its antiterrorist program will not eliminate the terrorist threat against Americans. Americans are prime terrorist targets for a variety of reasons ranging from their active participation in world economic and political affairs to their representation of a nation that most terrorists blame for their problems. These reasons coupled with the ability of the American media to cover world affairs offer terrorists the opportunity for publicity and recognition, and no matter how strident U.S. policy is, this will continue.

The public nature of the Reagan administration's antiterrorist stance represents a serious flaw in U.S. policy. International terrorists are weak political actors lacking the means to express their wants other than through the use of violence geared to generate publicity. By consistently drawing the media's and public's attention toward the issue of terrorism and individuals like Colonel Khaddafi, the administration is helping terrorists achieve recognition and legitimacy. Instead of deterring and reducing the terrorist phenomenon, the Reagan administration may be promoting terrorist behavior by providing a channel to the public for those groups seeking recognition.

The U.S. antiterrorist program should aim to reduce the effects of terrorism by not bringing the issue before the public on a regular basis. Instead, as pointed out by the ASIL's mid–1970s study on terrorism: "The U.S. government should de–emphasize the significance of the dangers and threats of terrorism. This policy would help prevent the creation of a climate of fear and apprehension among the general population. Emphasis on such dangers and the helplessness of society makes the psychological impact of terror–violence activities more effective and can induce terrorists to commit such acts."[42] The study also recommends, however, that "the U.S. should forthrightly condemn private and public measures of terror, whether engaged in at home or abroad by individuals or groups."[43] The study states that the goal of this policy should be to "help condition social expectation away from such terrorist activity" and "failure to do so might allow public attitudes to be shaped by the terrorists."[44]

There are no simple or one–dimensional solutions to international terrorism. The American response to terrorism must be comprised of not only military or diplomatic actions but of all of the foreign policy tools available and must balance the need to deal effectively with terrorism with the need to protect American civil liberties and the rights of other nationals.

NOTES

1.   U.S. Congress, Senate, Committee on Governmental Affairs, *An Act to Combat International Terrorism: Hearing on S. 2236*, 95th Cong., 2d sess., 27 January 1978, p. 138.

2.   U.S. Congress, House, Subcommittee on Civil and Constitutional Rights of the Committee on the Judiciary, *Federal Capabilities in Crisis Management and Terrorism*, 95th Cong., 2d sess., 16 August 1978, p. 57.

3.   Schlomo Gazit and Michael Handel, "Insurgency, Terrorism, and Intelligence," in *Intelligence Requirements for the 1980s: Counter–Intelligence*, ed. Roy Godson (Washington, D.C.: National Strategy Information Center, 1980), p. 130.

4.   "Secret Policy on Terrorism Given Airing," *The Washington Post*, 18 April 1984, p. A1.

5.   Ganzit and Handel, "Insurgency, Terrorism, and Intelligence," p. 131.

6.   U.S. President, Executive Order 12333, "United States Intelligence Activities," *Weekly Compilation of Presidential Documents* 17 (October–December 1981): 1336–1348 passim.

7.   U.S. Department of State, *Combatting Terrorism: American Policy and Organization*, Department of State Bulletin (August 1982), p. 6.

8.   U.S. Congress, House, Subcommittee on Civil and Constitutional Rights of the Committee on the Judiciary, *Federal Capabilities in Crisis Management and Terrorism*, 16 August 1978, p. 36.

9.   U.S. President, Executive Order 12333, p. 1348.

10.   Ibid., p. 1344.

11.   Ibid., p. 1338.

12.   U.S. Congress, Senate, Committee on Governmental Affairs, *An Act to Combat International Terrorism: Hearing on S. 2236*, 27 January 1978, p. 137.

13.   Neil C. Livingstone, *The War against Terrorism* (Lexington, Mass.: Lexington Books, 1982), p. 161.

14.   U.S. Department of State, *International Terrorism: Current Trends and the U.S. Response*, Bureau of Public Affairs' Circular no. 706. (Washington, D.C.: U.S. Department of State, Bureau of Public Affairs, Office of Communications, May 1985), p. 4.

15.   U.S. Congress, House, Subcommittee on Civil and Constitutional Rights of the Committee on the Judiciary, *Federal Capabilities in Crisis Management and Terrorism*, 16 August 1978, p. 57.

16.   Ibid.

17.   Robert E. Hunter, *Presidential Control of Foreign Policy: Management or Mishap?* The Washington Papers, no. 91 (New York: Praeger Publishers, 1982), p. 113.

18.   U.S. Department of State, *International Terrorism*, Bureau of Public Affairs Circular no. 706, p. 4.

19.   U.S. President, Executive Order 12333, p. 1347.

20. "Document: Statement by Senator Jeremiah Denton before the Subcommittee on Security and Terrorism, February 2, 1983," *Terrorism: An International Journal* 7, no. 1 (1983): 76.

21. U.S. President, Executive Order 12333, p. 1347.

22. Ibid., p. 1346.

23. Thomas H. Etzold and John Lewis Gaddis, *Containment: Documents on American Policy and Strategy, 19451950* (New York: Columbia University Press, 1978), p. 126.

24. U.S. Congress, House, Subcommittee on Civil and Constitutional Rights of the Committee on the Judiciary, *Federal Capabilities in Crisis Management and Terrorism*, 16 August 1978, p. 56.

25. U.S. Department of State, *International Terrorism*, Department of State Bulletin (August 1986), p. 3.

26. Abram Schulsky, "Discussion" of Schlomo Gazit and Michael Handel, "Insurgency, Terrorism, and Intelligence," in *Intelligence Requirements for the 1980s: Counter-Intelligence*, ed. Roy Godson (Washington, D.C.: National Strategy Information Center, 1980), p. 153.

27. U.S. Congress, House, Subcommittee on the Department of Defense of the Committee on Appropriations, *Department of Defense Appropriations for 1987: Special Operations Forces*, 99th Cong., 2d sess., 10 April 1986, p. 554.

28. U.S. Department of State, *International Terrorism*, Department of State Bulletin, p. 1.

29. U.S. Congress, Senate, Subcommittee on Foreign Assistance of the Committee on Foreign Relations, *International Terrorism*, 95th Cong., 1st sess., 14 September 1977, p. 72.

30. Ibid.

31. Yonah Alexander, ed., "Adequacy of U.S. Marine Corps Security in Beirut," *Terrorism: An International Journal* 7, no. 3 (1984): 343.

32. Anthony C. E. Quainton, "Terrorism: Policy, Action and Reaction," in *Perspectives on Terrorism*, ed. Lawrence Zelic Freedman and Yonah Alexander (Wilmington, Del.: Scholarly Resources, 1983), p. 176.

33. "Real and Illusionary Events," *Time* (October 13, 1986), p. 42.

34. U.S. President, Executive Order 12333, pp. 1336–1348 passim.

35. "CIA aides shuffled," *New Haven Register*, 28 June 1984, p. A1.

36. Wayne A. Kerstetter, "Terrorism and Intelligence," *Terrorism: An International Journal* 3, nos. 1–2 (1979): 111.

37. Edward A. Lynch, "International Terrorism: The Search for a Policy," *Terrorism: An International Journal* 9, no. 1 (1987): 2–3.

38. "Byrd Seeks Senate Probe of Charges of Report Altering at CIA," *The Washington Post*, 29 September 1984, p. A20.

39. Anthony C. E. Quainton, "Terrorism and Political Violence: A Permanent Challenge to Governments," in *Terrorism, Legitimacy, and Power: The Consequences of Political Violence*, ed. Martha Crenshaw (Middletown, Conn.: Wesleyan University Press, 1983), p. 57.

40. John F. Murphy, "State Self-Help and Problems of Public International Law," in *Legal Aspects of International Terrorism*, ed. Alona E. Evans and John F. Murphy (Lexington, Mass.: Lexington Books, 1978), p. 570.

41. Ernest Evans, *Calling a Truce to Terror: The American Response to International Terrorism* (Westport, Conn.: Greenwood Press, 1979), p. 121.

42. Alona E. Evans and John F. Murphy, eds., *Legal Aspects of International Terrorism* (Lexington, Mass.: Lexington Books, 1978), p. 659.

43. Ibid., p. 665.

44. Ibid.

7
American Use of International Law in Combatting Terrorism

On August 11, 1975, Secretary of State Henry A. Kissinger, in an address before the American Bar Association's Annual Convention in Montreal, stated:

> An international order can be neither stable nor just without accepted norms of conduct. International law both provides a means and embodies our ends. It is a repository of our experience and our idealism—a body of principles drawn from the practice of states and an instrument for fashioning new patterns of relations between states. Law is an expression of our own culture and yet a symbol of universal goals. It is the heritage of our past and a means of shaping our future.[1]

Kissinger's remarks represent the foundation of U.S. multilateral efforts to combat terrorism. International law and cooperation based on a stable international order using just norms of conduct represent a vital means of deterring and preventing the occurrence of terrorism and a key component of U.S. antiterrorist efforts.

The United States believes that terrorism "is a threat to human rights and to the basic right to civil peace and security which a society owes its citizens"[2] and the "norms that govern international relations."[3] To address the impact of terrorism, the United States views international initiatives and diplomacy as important "to discourage state support of terrorism and to build a broad consensus that terrorist acts are inadmissible under international law irrespective of the cause in which they are used."[4] In addition, as outlined by Ambassador Robert B. Oakley, former Ambassador-at-Large for Counterterrorism (designate), "only through long-term, cooperative international action can terrorist problems be reduced."[5] This chapter outlines the evolution of American attempts to employ international law, cooperation and organizations in combatting terrorism. To illustrate the difficulties associated with international efforts to combat terrorism, a brief examination of pre–World War II attempts to control terrorism is presented.

PRE–WORLD WAR II

While traveling through the streets of Marseilles, France, with French Foreign Minister Louis Barthou, King Alexander of Yugoslavia was assassinated on October 9, 1934. His assassination led to the presentation to the League of Nations of the

1937 Convention for the Creation of an International Criminal Court and the 1937 Convention for the Prevention and Punishment of Terrorism. On November 16, 1937, 24 of the 25 nations present at the League of Nations' conference in Geneva, Switzerland, signed both conventions.[6] The Geneva Convention of 1937 was the first universal international attempt to deal with terrorism. Before the formulation of the 1937 convention, only regional treaties and conventions had attempted to deal with terrorist behavior, such as the Mexico City Treaty of January 28, 1902, dealing with the extradition of criminals and protection under anarchism.[7]

The assassination of King Alexander acted as a catalyst in moving the international community toward dealing with terrorism on a much broader scale. Of the 25 nations assembled at the Geneva Conference of 1937, only 1 nation, India, ratified the Convention for the Prevention and Punishment of Terrorism; no nation ratified the Convention for the Creation of an International Criminal Court, and 1 nation, Great Britain, did not sign either convention. Great Britain opposed the Convention for the Prevention and Punishment of Terrorism because of its extremely broad definition of *terrorism,* which classified all forms of political behavior ranging from assassinations to dealings in the sale of arms and ammunition as terrorist behavior. The convention's all–encompassing definition irritated many of the more powerful nations of Western Europe. However, what stirred Great Britain's opposition was a provision of article 3 that required a signatory "to enact legislation to punish the incitement to commit terrorism."[8] Great Britain stated that article 3 would restrict "the free expression of public opinion which, especially in the political sphere, had for centuries been zealously safeguarded in Great Britain."[9] The rise to power of Hitler and the onset of World War II doomed any chance the conventions had of becoming legally binding components of international law.

CONTEMPORARY ERA

By the late 1960s, power relationships within international organizations like the United Nations were radically altered by the numerical dominance of the developing nations. Reaching agreements within international organizations on key issues ranging from international development assistance to international terrorism was a frustrating and complex process requiring luck, diplomatic skill and fragile coalitions. This made it virtually impossible to reach a consensus on how to deal with terrorism and political offenses.

The international community's first attempt in the post–World War II era at dealing with terrorism occurred in 1954. During the 1954 session of the United Nations, its International Law Commission drafted the Code of Offenses against the Peace and Security of Mankind. This code attempted to deal with terrorism by outlining the scope of political offenses. It stated that "the undertaking or encouragement by the authorities of a state of terrorist activities in another state, or the toleration by the authorities of a state of organized activities calculated to carry out terrorist acts in another state," constitute political offenses that are against the norms and standards of international conduct.[10] In addition to the code, an organizational framework for an International Criminal Court was formulated. Both proposals were submitted to the General Assembly. However, the Code of Offenses against the Peace and Security of Mankind was never brought to a vote because of the United Nations' inability to formulate a legal definition of *aggression.*[11]

In response to the Munich incident of September 5–6, 1972, Secretary General

Kurt Waldheim sought on September 8, 1972, the inclusion on the 27th session of the United Nations' General Assembly's agenda "an item entitled: 'Measures to prevent terrorist and other forms of violence which endanger or take innocent lives or jeopardize fundamental freedoms.'"[12] This action touched off a contentious debate within the United Nations. First, a number of Third World nations, through a proposal offered by Yemen, sought the deferment of the terrorism issue. On September 23, 1972, by a 57 to 47 vote, with 22 abstentions, Yemen's proposal was defeated. On the same day, the General Assembly adopted the Secretary General's request. However, the original request was modified by amendments proposed by Jamaica and Saudi Arabia and now included the "study of the underlying causes of those forms of terrorism, and acts of violence which lie in misery, frustration, grievance, and despair, and which cause some people to sacrifice human lives, including their own, in an attempt to effect radical changes."[13]

On September 24, 1972, Secretary of State Rogers, in an address entitled "A World Free of Violence," called on the United Nations to deal with terrorism directed toward diplomatic personnel, to take steps to deal with the export of international terrorism and to formulate a treaty suspending air service to nations aiding and/or abetting hijackers.[14] On the same day, the United States tabled a draft Convention for the Prevention and Punishment of Certain Acts of International Terrorism and a draft resolution for the U.N.'s Legal or Sixth Committee's consideration calling on "all states to become parties to the various international conventions on unlawful interference with civil aviation; to cooperate with each other to deter and prevent acts of international terrorism; and to convene a conference to consider the adoption of a convention on the prevention and punishment of international terrorism."[15]

The U.S. draft convention sought to deal with only specific acts of terrorism as outlined by Secretary Roger's address. The U.S. proposal contained no definition of *terrorism* and, as pointed out by U.S. Ambassador W. Tapley Bennett, Jr., before the Sixth Committee on November 13, 1972, was narrowly focused "on the common interest of all nations in preventing the spread of violence from areas involved in civil or international conflict or internal disturbances to countries not initially parties to the violence."[16] The draft convention sought to avoid the type of all-encompassing provisions that affected the Geneva Convention of 1937 and specifically excluded complex issues like wars of national liberation. Unfortunately, neither the U.S. draft resolution nor the convention gained much support. Instead, the Sixth Committee considered an Italian proposal, also known as the 14-Power Draft and supported by the United States, that "condemned acts of international terrorism, particularly those resulting in the loss of innocent lives; called for the drafting of a convention on measures to prevent international terrorism; and called for the establishment of a 32-member *ad hoc* committee to study the underlying causes of terrorism" and an Algerian proposal or 16-Power Draft.[17] The Algerian position was that national liberation movements must have a free hand; "that governmental actions cause death, so why should the international community single out acts of terrorists over any other political actor; that there can be no action taken against terrorism until the underlying causes of terrorism are eliminated; and that one cannot take action against terrorist groups without taking action against state terrorism."[18]

Incorporating a Saudi Arabian proposal to study the causes of terrorism, the General Assembly on December 18, 1972, voted 76 to 35, with 17 abstentions, to adopt the 16-Power Draft as U.N. Resolution 3034. The 14-Power Draft was never pressed to a vote, and the United States voted against the Algerian proposal on grounds that it failed to "deal directly with the question of measures to prevent international terrorism."[19] In addition, Ambassador Bennett has stated that the Algerian proposal was "defective in that it has made a political problem out of what to my delegation is essentially a human problem, a problem involving the right of every individual to the security of his person as promised him under the Declaration of Human Rights."[20]

U.N. Resolution 3034 was a major setback for the United States in its attempt to combat terrorism through multilateral efforts. However, since the early 1970s, the United States has still encouraged international antiterrorist efforts. American international efforts are based on the recognition of the difficulties associated with terrorism. This has led the United States to persuade the international community to deal with specific acts of terrorism, such as hijackings, instead of pushing for one convention embracing the entire concept of terrorism.

Air Terrorism

The first American initiative for dealing with a specific act of terrorism was the Convention on Offenses and Certain Other Acts Committed on Board Aircraft. This convention was adopted by the International Civil Aviation Organization (ICAO) on September 14, 1963 at its Tokyo conference. The Tokyo Convention of 1963 was signed by the United States on September 14, 1963, and approved by the U.S. Senate on June 30, 1969.[21] As of February 1986, 121 nations have become parties to this convention.[22] This convention is the foundation on which all other conventions dealing with terrorism affecting civil aviation have been based. Article 11 of the convention is the heart of the international community's attempt to deal with hijackings. It "requires member states to take all appropriate measures for returning a hijacked aircraft to the control of its commander and to facilitate the onward passage of the aircraft, crew and passengers after the hijacked aircraft has landed."[23]

The official American position on the Tokyo Convention was expressed on February 5, 1969, by Deputy Assistant Secretary of State for Transportation and Telecommunications Frank E. Loy. He stated before the House of Representatives' Committee on Interstate and Foreign Commerce that "aircraft hijackings are a most serious problem" and "that article 11 of the Tokyo Convention should be established as an internationally accepted norm."[24] Loy's concern over hijackings and its impact on civil aviation were well-founded. By the late 1960s, hijackings and other terrorist acts against civil aviation had reached epidemic levels. For the period between 1968 to the end of 1979, more than 55 percent of all hijackings had occurred between 1969 and the end of 1972.[25] In response to this problem, the ICAO adopted two more conventions dealing with this issue.

The next attempt to strengthen the international response to terrorism directed toward civil aviation was adopted by the ICAO's December 1970 conference at The Hague. On December 16, 1970, 50 of the 77 nations assembled at The Hague signed the Convention on the Suppression of Unlawful Seizure of Aircraft and as of February 1986, 126 nations have ratified it.[26] The United States signed the convention on December 16, 1970, and ratified it on September 13, 1971.[27] The United States has supported this convention for a number of reasons. First, the convention serves notice that hijacking, whatever the motivation, is universally considered a serious common crime and not a political offense. Second, articles 7 and 8 of the convention serve as a deterrent to hijacking because they require member states either to extradite the hijacker to another state for prosecution or prosecute the hijacker themselves.[28] The Hague Convention also amended all existing extradition treaties, including 76 of the 80 bilateral extradition treaties the United States had in force at the time, to include hijacking as an extraditable offense.[29]

Following The Hague Convention, the ICAO on September 23, 1971, adopted the Convention on the Suppression of Unlawful Acts against the Safety of Civil Aviation. This convention was signed at the ICAO's Montreal meeting by 27 of the attending nations, and as of February 1986, 127 nations, including the United States, had ratified the Montreal Convention of 1971.[30]

The United States supported this convention because it believed that it, coupled with the Tokyo Convention of 1963 and The Hague Convention of 1970, represented the needed groundwork on which more extensive international actions against terrorism could be launched.[31] At the heart of the Montreal Convention are the provisions outlined in articles 1 and 8. Article 1 covers the series of offenses that could be carried out against all aspects of air transportation. The article covers violence against passengers, crews, destruction or damage of air navigation facilities and the interference with aeronautical communications.[32] Article 8 specifies the convention's extradition provisions and requirements and "also provides that offenses shall be extraditable offenses between states which do not make extradition conditional on an extradition treaty."[33]

The Tokyo Convention, The Hague Convention and the Montreal Convention represent the core of the first international attempt to deal with one specific form of terrorism. The United States has attempted to build on the groundwork constructed by these conventions. The first attempt was associated with the draft Convention for the Prevention and Punishment of Certain Acts of International Terrorism. The convention contained a proposal to suspend air service to nations determined to be aiding and/or abetting hijackers. But as outlined above, this draft convention has never been considered by the United Nations.

However, U.S. bilateral efforts of the 1970s did produce results. The U.S.-Cuban Memorandum of Understanding on Hijacking of Aircraft and Vessels and Other Offenses, signed on February 15, 1973, by Secretary of State Rogers and Joroslav Zantovsky, Chargé d'Affairs of Czechoslovakia, representing Cuba, demonstrates the utility of cooperative measures in combatting terrorism.[34] This memorandum of understanding, coupled with three others formulated between Cuba and Mexico, Venezuela and Columbia and the security measures mandated by the Air Transportation Security Act of 1974 have been credited with the drastic curtailment of hijackings occurring within U.S. airspace and in South and North American airspace in general.[35] Between 1973 (after the signing of the bilateral agreement with Cuba) and 1979, only 12 hijackings occurred within U.S. airspace compared with 37 that took place from 1968 to 1973.[36] Unfortunately, the agreement between the United States and Cuba has expired, and because of the extremely poor state of relations between the two nations, the agreement most likely will not be renewed.

Between August 28 and September 23, 1973, an extraordinary assembly of the ICAO was convened in Rome. The assembly was convened in the hope that the momentum established by the Montreal and The Hague Conventions could be maintained and furthered. The United States strongly supported a proposal brought before the assembly calling for "an independent convention which would enable international scrutiny and moral pressure to be brought to bear upon states acting contrary to the principles of The Hague and Montreal Conventions."[37] Specifically, the United States and other nations sought an agreement that would impose sanctions on those nations determined to be aiding and/or abetting hijackers, which "included the possible suspension of all international air navigation to and from the violating state."[38] The proposed convention was opposed by France and the Soviet

Union on the grounds that "international sanctions could not be imposed except by the U.N. Security Council under Article VII of the U.N. Charter."[39] French and Soviet opposition was enough to kill the proposed convention.

The international commmunity throughout the mid–1970s and early 1980s was unable to build on the groundwork created by the Tokyo, The Hague and Montreal Conventions. However, in response to the June 1985 hijacking of TWA Flight 847, in which U.S. Navy diver Robert Stethem was executed and 39 American men were held prisoner for 13 days, Secretary of Transportation Elizabeth Dole, in June 1985, called on the ICAO to "review security measures as they are currently implemented by member nations with a view toward improving security at international airports; to review and, where necessary, strengthen existing international airport security standards; to provide a means for evaluating the level of adherence to ICAO security standards at international airports; and to expand its security training program."[40] Acting on Dole's request, the ICAO in December 1985 revised and strengthened the security standards outlined by Annex 17 of the 1944 Convention on International Civil Aviation, or the Chicago Convention. On February 1986, while appearing before a joint hearing of the House of Representatives' Subcommittee on Arms Control, International Security and Science and on International Operations of the Committee on Foreign Affairs and the Subcommittee on Aviation of the Committee on Public Works and Transportation, Assistant Secretary of Transportation for Policy and International Affairs Matthew V. Scocozza outlined the changes to Annex 17. He stated that member nations of the ICAO were now required to "expand preflight checks to include measures to discover weapons and other dangerous devices; ensure that baggage that does not belong to any boarded passenger is either not loaded or is thoroughly inspected; and enhance other safeguards at international airports and ground facilities" and recommended "that countries include a clause on civil aviation security in their aviation agreements with other nations."[41] In addition, the ICAO has continued work on ways to enhance its organizational approach to aviation security, its technical assistance to member nations and "the formulation of standard procedures for countries to use to evaluate their own security program."[42]

Diplomats, Hostage Taking and Terrorism

One of the most rapidly developing trends of terrorist activity has been the increase in kidnappings and violence directed against diplomatic personnel. The first multilateral attempt at dealing with this form of terrorism took place on February 2, 1971. In response to the spreading epidemic of attacks directed against diplomatic personnel in general and the murder of the German ambassador to Guatemala in particular, the United States on April 15, 1970, called on the Organization of American States (OAS) to address this issue.[43] The first signs of disagreement within the contemporary international community over the issue of terrorism surfaced during the OAS meeting of early 1971. During the debate and formulation of the Washington Convention, the United States chose not to address the general concept of terrorism, particularly terrorism by dissidents against the governments in power. Argentina, Brazil, Ecuador and Paraguay objected to this exclusion. These four nations and two others, some of whose governments were being threatened by terrorism, walked out of the Washington Conference and did not sign the convention.[44]

On February 2, 1971, in Washington, 13 members of the OAS, including the United States, signed the "Convention to Prevent and Punish the Acts of Terrorism

Taking the Form of Crimes against Persons of International Significance."[45] The Washington Convention of 1971 was ratified by the United States on October 8, 1976, and entered into force on October 20, 1976.[46] Concerning this treaty, President Ford, on October 20, 1976, stated that "an important factor of this treaty will be to give extraterritorial effect to our law in order to enable us to punish those who commit offenses against internationally protected persons, wherever these offenses may occur."[47]

The United Nations, due to Yugoslav interest, also formulated a convention attempting to protect diplomatic personnel. On December 14, 1973, the United Nations adopted the "Convention on the Prevention and Punishment of Crimes against Internationally Protected Persons, Including Diplomatic Agents."[48] The New York Convention of 1973 was signed by the United States on December 28, 1973, and ratified on the same day as the Washington Convention of 1971.[49] These two conventions, however, have not deterred or prevented terrorist attacks against such individuals. Between 1976 and 1979, 99 terrorist incidents took place involving diplomatic personnel and installations. This is a decrease from the period of 1973 to 1975 in which 100 such incidents occurred.[50] The trend, however, in terrorist attacks against diplomatic personnel and institutions was radically altered in 1980. In 1980, more than 400 terrorist attacks were carried out against diplomatic personnel; Americans were involved in 100 of these assaults.[51] The most vivid illustrations of this trend were the assaults against American embassies and diplomatic posts in Iran, Pakistan and Libya and more recently in Kuwait and Lebanon.

On April 24, 1975, six members of the Socialist Patients' Collective seized the West German Embassy in Stockholm, Sweden, along with 11 hostages including the West German Ambassador to Sweden, Dieter Stoecker. During the siege, the terrorists executed the West German military attaché, Lieutenant Colonel Andreas Baron von Mirach. The siege ended on midnight of April 24 with the accidental explosion of the terrorists' own explosives.[52] In response to this incident, West German Foreign Minister Genscher called on the United Nations on September 28, 1976, "to draft an international convention against the taking of hostages."[53]

The United Nations accepted the West German call to formulate a convention on the taking of hostages, and on December 17, 1979, it adopted the "Convention against the Taking of Hostages." The formulation and adoption of this convention marks a watershed in the international community's willingness to tackle the difficult issues associated with terrorism.

The New York Convention of 1979 is a milestone in the international community's antiterrorist efforts because of the hurdles that were overcome in its formulation.[54] During the four-year debate that led to this convention, the same issues that were raised during the 27th session of the United Nations in 1972 were present. On one side of the debate, Western European-oriented nations such as West Germany and the United States believed the most important issue to be considered was "the principle of 'prosecute or extradite.'"[55] On the other side, Third World and Eastern European nations raised questions concerning national liberation movements, asylum and an "anti-Entebbe" clause.[56]

During the four-year debate over these issues, West Germany, not the United States, exercised the leadership role. West Germany dealt with each issue individually, and its leadership has been cited as one of the main reasons for the successful formulation and adoption of this convention. This factor, coupled with a changing attitude within the international community, even within the Third World, enabled the Western European-oriented nations to prevail on the main issues.[57]

The heart of the New York Convention of 1979 is article 12. The essence of this article, in the words of former Under Secretary of State for Management John Kennedy, is the legal obligation of the signatories to either "extradite or submit to their competent authorities for prosecution alleged hostage-takers found within their jurisdictions." In addition, a state "must comply with this obligation without regard to where the alleged hostage-taking was committed," and signatories are required "to cooperate in preventing hostage-taking by means of internal protective measures, exchange of information and coordination of enforcement activities."[58] U.S. Ambassador John W. McDonald, of the State Department's Bureau of International Organization Affairs, has characterized the main feature of the New York Convention as signifying that there are "no longer 'safe havens' in the participating nations for terrorist hostage-takers."[59]   By September 1982, 40 nations had signed this convention, and 18 of them had ratified it, including the United States.[60]

Extradition and Terrorism

One of the most important set of issues dealing with terrorism is associated with the prosecution and/or extradition of those individuals charged with engaging in terrorist activity. The extradition and/or prosecution provision is viewed by the United States as the heart of all international agreements and conventions dealing with terrorism. The extradition and the prosecution of terrorists and the acceptance by nations of this duty is viewed as vital to the elimination of safe havens for terrorists and the deterrence of terrorism.[61]   Henry Kissinger has stated that "if all nations deny terrorists a safe haven, terrorists' practices will be substantially reduced."[62]

However, the international community lacks a convention embracing the ideal of universal jurisdiction for the extradition of persons charged with committing terrorist acts. The Montevideo Convention of 1933 and the European Convention on the Suppression of Terrorism of 1976 do address this issue. However, both conventions lack the universality needed to deal with terrorism. For this reason the major conventions dealing with specific acts of terrorism, like The Hague Convention of 1970, have incorporated "a legal duty either to prosecute or extradite offenders who have committed the crime specified in the convention."[63]   Each major convention dealing with a specific act of terrorism has left to the nations becoming parties to these conventions the responsibility of modifying their extradition procedures. The United States through the use of bilateral agreements, has attempted to fulfill the extradition provisions outlined in the conventions to which it is a signatory. The United States as of February 1979 had formulated and adopted extradition agreements with 93 nations.[64]

The United States has traditionally viewed terrorist acts as common crimes. This perception outlines, possibly, the only feasible means of combatting terrorism and, because of the differing views of terrorism, the only way to extradite and prosecute terrorists. American extradition efforts have been confronted by a number of considerations. The first is domestic political considerations. An example was the recent debate within the Senate's Foreign Relations Committee over the formulation of a new extradition treaty with Great Britain. Concerned with the political power of the Irish-American community, a number of senators, mainly Senators Kerry (D-Mass.) and Biden (D-Del.), opposed the extradition treaty. Only after the Reagan administration made it clear that it considered the treaty an important tool in combatting terrorism, and fearing "accusations that they were insufficiently vigilant against terrorism," did members of the Foreign

Relations Committee reach a compromise and pass the treaty onto the full Senate for a vote.[65]

Another and perhaps more complex consideration confronting U.S. extradition efforts is political asylum. The ability to extend asylum has been viewed by many states as an expression of sovereignty. France has been the most forceful nation in denying extradition requests and has also frequently extended political asylum to suspected terrorists. One of the most frustrating examples of French refusal to extradite a suspected terrorist(s) is the Holder case.[66] On June 3, 1972, William Roger Holder and Katherine Mary Kerkow hijacked Western Airline flight 701 traveling from Los Angeles to Seattle. After receiving their ransom demands, Holder and Kerkow ordered the aircraft to fly to Algeria. On arrival in Algeria both hijackers were placed under house arrest and the money received during the hijacking was returned. Because of Holder's association with the Black Panthers and the Algerian government's classification of the Black Panthers as a liberation movement, neither hijacker was sent back to the United States. During his time in Algeria, Holder became involved in a power struggle within the Black Panther Organization based in Algeria, which led to its breakup. Thereafter, Holder and Kerkow traveled to Paris, where they were arrested on January 24, 1975.[67] The United States, which has an extradition treaty with France, requested their extradition, but a French court refused the request. The court's decision was based on legal and political considerations extending from France's views on the meaning of political offenses.[68]

Nuclear Power and Terrorism

Lewis A. Dunn, a member of the Hudson Institute, in an article entitled "Nuclear Proliferation and World Politics," stated that "further contributing to the erosion of global order would be the spreading of nuclear terrorism."[69] His fears associated with nuclear terrorism have been recognized by the international community. Under pressure from the United States, the International Atomic Energy Agency (IAEA) in 1974 began an examination into the problems of nuclear proliferation and the theft of nuclear materials and their relationship to terrorist activity. Between 1977 and 1979, the IAEA drafted the Convention on the Physical Protection of Nuclear Material.[70] The United States signed the convention in Vienna on March 3, 1980, and ratified it during 1982.[71]

The core articles of the Vienna Convention are article 3 and 7 to 14. Article 3 "requires states party to the treaty to take steps to protect nuclear material according to technical standards set forth in the annexes to the agreement" and also states that nations "are required to take special precautions with receivers and senders of such materials, including protection by escorts in touch with response forces."[72] Articles 7 through 14 require "states to make such offenses as theft of nuclear materials, nuclear threats by terrorists punishable under their laws."[73] These articles also state that a state "shall either prosecute the offenders or extradite them for prosecution."[74] The Vienna Convention represents a positive step in dealing with the threat of nuclear terrorism. More than 35 nations are currently parties to this convention, including all of the nuclear powers except China.[75] However, the question of the theft of a nuclear weapon has still to be addressed by the international community.

Maritime Terrorism

On October 7, 1985, four terrorists seized the Achille Lauro, an Italian cruise ship, off the coast of Egypt. The terrorists took approximately 400 passengers and crew hostage, including 12 Americans. During the incident the terrorists brutally killed Leon Klinghoffer, a wheelchaired American, and dumped his body overboard. As pointed out by U.S. Ambassador Robert Oakley, this incident caught many nations off guard and "jolted the U.S. and other governments into a much more active policy of safety standards for ships and ports."[76]

Acting upon a U.S. resolution calling for the development of measures to prevent "terrorist attacks against passengers and crews on board ships," the International Maritime Organization (IMO), in November 1985, instructed the Maritime Safety Committee (MSC) to take up this issue. By the fall of 1986, the IMO, with the necessary modifications to make it suitable for application to the Maritime situation, is expected to adopt a U.S. proposal for maritime security procedures patterned after the international civil aviation security requirements outlined in Annex 17 of the 1944 Chicago Convention. The U.S. proposal calls for the establishment of a Ship Security Plan and Port Security Plan. These plans are called for in the hope of providing "for the inspection, screening, and security of passengers, baggage, cargo and ship stores" so as "to prevent the introduction of firearms, weapons and other dangerous devices onto the ship and ship embarkation areas."[77] It is hoped that the IMO's prompt response to the Achille Lauro will deter and prevent any future attempt to hijack a cruiseliner.

Regional Declarations and Terrorism

The mid-1970s study by the American Society of International Law (ASIL), for the Department of State on the American response to terrorism, recommended a number of steps designed to enhance the U.S. and the international community's application of international law and cooperation in combatting terrorism. One recommendation supported the formulation of "a single convention on legal control of international terrorism, to be drafted in a conference held outside the auspices of the United Nations."[78] The United States has rejected this recommendation. A second recommendation of the ASIL study, one that has been adopted and incorporated into the U.S. response to terrorism, was the call for a regional approach to the problem.[79]

Although not seeking to formulate regional conventions, the United States has attempted to establish a consensus on the need to deal with terrorism as expressed through regional declarations. This effort has required the participation of the nations of Western Europe and other industrialized democracies. The first regionally formulated and adopted declaration was the July 17, 1978, Bonn Economic Summit Declaration on Hijacking. On July 17, 1978, Canada, France, West Germany, Italy, Japan, the United States and the United Kingdom signed the Bonn Declaration, which stated that they would take immediate actions against any nation that aids and/or abets hijackers or fails to extradite or prosecute a hijacker. These nations also agreed to cease all flights to and from a nation that meets the above criteria.[80] Ambassador Anthony Quainton, former Director of the Department of State's Office for Combatting Terrorism, has hailed the Bonn Declaration as the "first multilateral enforcement mechanism against countries which condone acts of terrorism."[81]

Following the Bonn Declaration, the European Community, from the summer of 1980 to the winter of 1984, adopted eight more declarations or statements on terrorism.[82] Overall, each pronouncement has expressed concern with the increasingly violent nature and occurrence of terrorism and the need for effective cooperation and measures to deter, prevent and suppress terrorist activity. However, these statements lack specific provisions on how to combat terrorism, and as a CIA research paper on international terrorism stated, "little measurable action has resulted from any of these declarations, although the meetings in which the declarations were formulated continue to serve as a useful forums for exchanging information and reaching tentative agreements on international terrorism."[83] Yet the United States has continued to press for regional statements, and perhaps the most sought-after and comprehensive of regional documents is the May 1986 Tokyo Summit declaration. Determined to reinforce its pressure on Libya, the Reagan administration sought to get from the United States' six major allies a unified statement demonstrating a hard line against states, mainly the Khaddafi regime, aiding and/or abetting international terrorism. Unlike preceding declarations, this declaration outlined a number of specific antiterrorist actions, such as setting "limits on the size of diplomatic delegations of governments determined of supporting terrorism, more stringent extradition arrangements and a refusal to permit entry of any person expelled from another country for terrorist activities."[84] The Reagan administration was very pleased with the declaration and the unity demonstrated by its allies.

The European community has responded to the American call for declarations against terrorism. However, for these statements to be effective, the European community and the United States must recognize that not one or a series of statements will deter or prevent terrorism. Only a determined long-term commitment will have a positive impact on the suppression of terrorism.

The Reagan Administration

The Reagan administration views multilateral and bilateral efforts as useful instruments in combatting terrorism. The administration's multilateral efforts are, as outlined Parker W. Borg, Deputy, Office of the Ambassador-at-Large for Counterterrorism, designed in the hope of "increasing public understanding and awareness of the nature of terrorism; encouraging the development of internationally accepted standards of behavior and responsibility for individual states in preventing, deterring and punishing terrorism; and encouraging effective international cooperation to combat terrorism, including adherence to existing international counter-terrorism conventions."[85] Unfortunately, the administration, although encouraged by recent actions by the International Civil Aviation Organization, the International Maritime Organization and the U.N.'s Security Council, has, in general, viewed multilateral antiterrorism efforts as a weak alternative to bilateral efforts. This can best be illustrated by Ambassador Robert Oakley's comments about the conventions dealing with hijacking and hostage taking made before the House Subcommittee on International Operations on October 30, 1985. He stated that:

These international conventions are important because of the moral force they offer. Their effectiveness is limited, however, by the willingness or ability of states to enforce them. The existence of these conventions by themselves has not halted hijackings, crimes against diplomats, or hostage taking. As with extradition treaties, obtaining a country's ratification of a convention or treaty is one thing. Obtaining adherence is something else.[86]

The Reagan administration currently views the formulation and adoption of another convention dealing with any aspect of terrorism as redundant. Although it will support efforts such as the revising of Annex 17 of the 1944 Chicago Convention, the administration views those antiterrorism conventions already adopted as adequate and seeks to use both international law and the domestic criminal statutes of those nations involved in handling a terrorist incident as a means of deterring, preventing and suppressing terrorism.[87]

Due to the weaknesses of multilateral antiterrorism efforts, the Reagan administration has placed heavy emphasis on bilateral efforts. Bilateral efforts are viewed as the most effective means of dealing with terrorism because this approach allows the United States and other nations to face the problem "together, sharing information, protecting better each other's diplomatic facilities and developing common plans of action."[88] Perhaps the most sufficient bilateral effort is the before-mentioned Antiterrorism Assistance Program. This program has trained more than 1,500 civilian officials from 32 friendly foreign governments during the first two years of its existence. This program, coupled with other bilateral efforts such as those dealing with the exchange of intelligence, is a part of a U.S. effort, currently involving 50 governments, of constructing a "framework of multistate bilateral cooperation."[89]

The chief asset of bilateral efforts is that they allow the United States to formulate agreements, such as the 1970's U.S.–Cuban Memorandum of Understanding on Hijackings, with those nations that for some reason are unwilling to support U.S. antiterrorism efforts presented in more public international forums. However, bilateral efforts must be one component of a two–component U.S. effort to formulate an international consensus on the need to combat terrorism. Terrorism is a universal problem requiring universal cooperation if it is to be deterred, prevented and suppressed. The Reagan administration, unlike its predecessors, however, is not seeking to build on past multilateral efforts in its very public war against terrorism. Instead, the administration, while still supportive of past international antiterrorist efforts, appears to view much of international law and some international organizations with hostility—or with resigned indifference. The administration's refusal to accept the International Court of Justice's decision that Nicaragua can bring a case against the United States for its mining of Nicaraguan ports and support of the Contras' efforts to overthrow the present regime in Nicaragua and, then, its walkout and boycott of court proceedings is an important example of the administration's open hostility.[90] If international law and attempts at combatting terrorism are to be viable, the concept of international law and organizations must be supported by all nations, including the United States. If the Reagan administration decides to support only select parts of international law, its efforts in combatting terrorism will continue to be frustrated by a double standard that it also practices.

COMMENTS AND CONCLUSION

The American use of various types of international cooperation in combatting terrorism has a number of weaknesses. International cooperation is vital in the deterrence and prevention of terrorism. The key to the development of this cooperation is the formulation of an international consensus on the need to address this problem and how to do so.

The international community, as witnessed by the adoption of numerous antiterrorist conventions, has developed a growing degree of awareness and consensus on the need to combat terrorist behavior. However, this awareness or consensus is neither concrete nor universal. This has led to the United States' adoption of other methods and measures of formulating a consensus, such as regionalism. The regional approach, while establishing a regional consensus, is also working against the development of an international one. Those nations taking part in the U.S. regional efforts are, for the most part, representative of Western Europe and the industrialized–developed world. This factor might contribute to the polarization of the international community along economic lines and, thus, works against an effective international response to terrorism. Further undermining American bilateral and regional efforts at combatting terrorism is the disclosure of the Reagan administration's hypocritical behavior by the Iran arms–for–hostages affair. The Reagan administration had criticized its allies for dealing with those organizations and nations accused of aiding and/or abetting terrorists in the hope of gaining the release of hostages, yet at the same time, the administration was doing exactly that. This type of behavior has both angered and confused U.S. allies. It has undermined not only allied confidence in U.S. antiterrorist efforts, but also American leadership as it relates to other key international issues.

The most striking weakness of international law dealing with terrorism is its lack of enforceability. An illustration is the American use of the International Court of Justice during the Iranian hostage crisis. The United States won its case, and the court ordered the release of the hostages. The vast majority of the nations of the international community supported the American position and the court's decision. However, the United Nations Security Council, the court's executive arm, lacked the means and will to back the court's decision. The American hostages were released because of the diplomatic efforts of the Carter administration and the changing political environment in both Iran and the United States. It must be pointed out, however, that the Carter administration never believed the International Court of Justice's decision would change the status of the hostages. Yet U.S. use of the court and the U.N. Security Council demonstrated to Iran that it stood alone, and until the hostages were released, it would be unable to get the international community to focus on any issue it sought addressed.

Hence we have the resort to the doctrine of self–help. Great Britain, Israel, Egypt and West Germany have all taken unilateral military actions to combat terrorism, some of them successful, some of them not. These actions, coupled with the U.S. raid on Libya and the adoption of National Security Decision Directive (NSDD) 138, raise serious questions, chiefly about the legality of forceful self–help measures.

The debate over the use of force is divided, with "the crucial line to be drawn between the use of force in self–defense and the use of force by way of reprisal."[91] On July 3, 1976, four C–130 Hercules cargo aircraft, loaded with members of Israel's General Intelligence and Reconnaissance Unit 269, assaulted the Entebbe Airport in Uganda in a brilliant and daring hostage–rescue operation. Within 90 minutes the Israeli commandos and the rescued hostages were airborne and heading to Kenya and safety. In a matter of days the U.N. Security Council, under pressure from African nations through the Organization for African Unity, took up the issue of Israel's use of force in the rescue operation. Benin, Libya and Tanzania sought to have the Security Council adopt a resolution condemning Israel's behavior as a "flagrant violation of Uganda's sovereignty and territorial integrity."[92] In opposition were Israel and the United States. Israel stated that Uganda's violation of The Hague Convention of 1970 and its failure to protect foreign nationals justified the use of force to rescue the hostages as outlined by the doctrine of self–defense.[93] The United States supported Israel's position; however, it also restated its support for "the principle of territorial sovereignty."[94] The U.N. Security Council at the conclusion of the debate over Israel's action, mid–July 1976, did not adopt a formal position, and the African states' resolution was never pushed to a vote.

The Israeli act of July 3, 1976, while a violation of Uganda's sovereignty, can be morally and legally justified by Uganda's failure to execute its international legal obligations in protecting foreign nationals and its support of terrorism. Rescue operations such as Israel's are justified under the doctrine of self–defense and the rule of proportionality as long as there are exceptional and unique circumstances: the possible execution of hostages, the failure of or lack of effort by a nation to rescue hostages and the perception that foreign officials are aiding and/or abetting the terrorists' efforts. However, reprisals against subversive centers are condemned by international law. Drawing upon articles 2(3), 2(4) and 51 of the U.N. Charter, several Security Council resolutions and the writings of eminent jurists, John F. Murphy, Professor of Law at the University of Kansas School of Law, concluded "that reprisals involving the use or threat of force are illegal."[95] The difference between rescue operations and reprisals against subversive centers is a matter of scope and interpretation. Rescue operations are, one hopes, designed to rescue hostages successfully. Reprisals are designed to punish a nation for its aiding and/or abetting of terrorism, to compel it to make reparations to those states injured by terrorist behavior and/or to prevent further support of terrorism.

Finally, the Reagan administration's efforts to work out an aggressive policy toward terrorism and its supporters faces the important question of what if a state is not supporting a terrorist groups' actions, but the terrorists are using its territory? An example would be present–day Lebanon. The government of Lebanon lacks the means to police its own territory, and this places in doubt the utility of NSDD 138. The focus of NSDD 138 is too narrow and confining. It deals with terrorism as a form of state behavior. However, not all terrorism is tied to the behavior of a state, such as Libya. If NSDD 138 is to be effective, it must deal with terrorism on a wider scale.

A decision to use self–help measures to combat terrorism must take into account the numerous hazards associated with such methods. Counterintelligence operations, special activities and special operations are important tools in the war against terrorism. However, it must be recognized that the political, legal and moral price to be paid for this type of policy may be high. Also, the Reagan administration must be aware of the negative impact past abuses by the intelligence community have had on the image of the United States and on U.S. intelligence capabilities and their possible re–occurrence if the use of an aggressive policy against terrorism is not closely monitored and properly used.

The formulation of an international consensus on the need to combat terrorism is vital. United States' attempts to influence the international community to take actions against terrorist behavior have had some successes. However, the United States has had to face the reality that the international community is made up of many diverse nations, each seeking to protect and promote its own interests. For the United States to deal effectively with terrorism, it must recognize this reality.

NOTES

1. Henry A. Kissinger, *American Foreign Policy* (New York: W. W. Norton & Company, 1977), p. 219.

2. U.S. Department of State, *Human Rights and the Moral Dimension of U.S. Foreign Policy*, Department of State Bulletin (April 1984), p. 17.

3. U.S. Department of State, *Third Special Session of the OAS General Assembly Adopts Measures on Kidnapping and Terrorism*, Department of State Bulletin (February 22, 1971), p. 229.

4. U.S. National Security Council, *The United States Government Antiterrorism Program: An Unclassified Summary Report* (Washington, D.C.: Executive Committee on Terrorism of the Special Coordination Committee of the National Security Council, June 1979), p. 2.

5. U.S. Department of State, *Combatting International Terrorism*, Department of State Bulletin (June 1985), p. 74.

6. Robert H. Kupperman and Darell Trent, *Terrorism: Threat, Reality, Response* (Stanford, Calif.: Hoover Institution Press, 1979), p. 142.

7. Yonah Alexander, Marjorie Ann Browne, and Allan S. Nanes, *Control of Terrorism: International Documents* (New York: Crane, Russak & Company, 1979), p. 3.

8. John Dugard, "International Terrorism: Problems of Definition," *International Affairs* (Great Britain) 50 (January 1974): 69.

9. Ibid.

10. Kupperman and Trent, *Terrorism*, p. 142.

11. Ibid.

12. Thomas M. Franck and Bert B. Lockwood, Jr., "Preliminary Thoughts Towards an International Convention on Terrorism," *American Journal of International Law* (January 1974): 71.

13. U.S. Congress, House, Committee on Internal Security, *Terrorism, Part 2*, 93rd Cong., 2d sess., 16 May 1974, p. 3310.

14. U.S. Department of State, *A World Free of Violence*, Department of State Bulletin (October 16, 1972), p. 425.

15. U.S. Congress, House, Committee on Internal Security, *Terrorism, Part 2*, p. 3310.

16. U.S. Department of State, *U.S. Votes against U.N. General Assembly Resolution Calling for Study of Terrorism*, Department of State Bulletin (January 22, 1973), p. 83.

17. U.S. Congress, House, Committee on Internal Security, *Terrorism, Part 2*, p. 3310.

18. U.S. Department of State, *U.S. Calls for Responsible Measures against International Terrorism*, Department of State Bulletin (January 24, 1974), p. 76.

19. U.S. Congress, House, Committee on Internal Security, *Terrorism, Part 2*, p. 3310.

20. U.S. Department of State, *U.S. Votes*, p. 90.

21. Alexander, Browne, and Nanes, *Control of Terrorism*, p. 45.

22. U.S. Department of State, *International Terrorism*, Department of State Bulletin (August 1986), p. 8.

23. U.S. Department of State, *Department Reviews Problem of Aircraft Hijacking and Proposals for International Action*, Department of State Bulletin (March 10, 1969), p. 213.

24. Ibid.

25. Central Intelligence Agency, *International Terrorism in 1979*, National Foreign Assessment Center, Research Paper (1980), p. 16.

26. U.S. Department of State, *International Terrorism*, p. 8.

27. Alexander, Browne, and Nanes, *Control of Terrorism*, p. 55.

28. U.S. Department of State, *International Conference on Air Law Approves Convention on Aircraft Hijacking*, Department of State Bulletin (January 11, 1971), p. 50.

29. U.S. Department of State, *Department Urges Senate Advice and Consent to Ratification of Hijacking Convention*, Department of State Bulletin (July 1971), p. 87.

30. U.S. Department of State, *International Terrorism*, p. 8.

31. U.S. Department of State, *Department Urges Senate Advice and Consent to Ratification of Montreal Convention on Aviation Sabotage*, Department of State Bulletin (October 16, 1972), p. 448.

32. Ibid., pp. 446–448.

33. Ibid.

34. U.S. Department of State, *United States and Cuba Reach Agreement on Hijacking*, Department of State Bulletin (March 5, 1973), pp. 260–262.

35. Robert G. Bell, "The U.S. Response to Terrorism against International Civil Aviation," *Orbis* 19 (Winter 1976): 1326–1343 passim.

36. Central Intelligence Agency, *International Terrorism in 1979*, p. 16.

37. U.S. Department of State, *U.S. Pledges Continued Efforts for Aviation Security*, Department of State Bulletin (October 29, 1973), pp. 550–551.

38. Kupperman and Trent, *Terrorism*, p. 143.

39. Ibid., pp. 143–144.

40. U.S. Congress, House, Subcommittee on Arms Control, International Security and Science and on International Operations of the Committee on Foreign Affairs and the Subcommittee on Aviation of the Committee on Public Works and Transportation, *Joint Hearings: Impact of International Terrorism on Travel*, 99th Cong., 2d sess., 19 February 1986, p. 37.

41. Ibid., pp. 37–38.

42. Ibid., p.39.

43. U.S. Department of State, *OAS Asked to Consider Problem of Kidnapping and Terrorism*, Department of State Bulletin (May 25, 1970), p. 662.

44. Dugard, "International Terrorism," pp. 71–72.

45. U.S. Department of State, *Third Special Session*, pp. 228–234 passim.

46. U.S. Department of State, *President Ford Signs Ratification of Convention on Terrorism*, Department of State Bulletin (November 1976), p. 554.

47. Ibid.

48. Alexander, Browne, and Nanes, *Control of Terrorism*, p. 77.

49. U.S. Department of State, *President Ford Signs Ratification*, p. 554.

50. Central Intelligence Agency, *International Terrorism in 1979*, p. 16.

51. U.S. Department of State, *The Impact of International Terrorism*, Department of State Bulletin (January 1982), p. 56.

52. Edward F. Mickolus, *Transnational Terrorism: A Chronology of Events, 1968–1979* (Westport, Conn.: Greenwood Press, 1980), pp. 518–519.

53. Ambassador John W. McDonald, Jr., "The United Nations Convention against the Taking of Hostages: The Inside Story," *Terrorism: An International Journal* 6, no. 4 (1983): 546.

54. Ibid., p. 558.

55. Ibid., p. 548.

56. Ibid., pp. 548–549.

57. Ibid., p. 559.

58. U.S. Congress, Senate, Committee on Foreign Relations, *International Terrorism: Hearings on S. 873*, 97th Cong., 1st sess., 10 June 1981, p. 40.

59. McDonald, "The United Nations Convention Against the Taking of Hostages," p. 558.

60. Ibid.

61. U.S. Department of State, *The Role of International Law in Combatting Terrorism*, Current Foreign Policy Series, no. 8689 (Washington, D.C.: U.S. Government Printing Office, 1973), p. 2.

62. Kissinger, *American Foreign Policy*, p. 232.

63. Burns H. Weston, Richard A. Falk, and Anthony A. D'Amato, *International Law and World Order: A Problem-Oriented Coursebook* (St. Paul, Minn.: West Publishing Company, 1983), p. 495.

64. U.S. Congress, House, Subcommittee on Aviation of the Committee on Public Works and Transportation, *Aircraft Piracy, International Terrorism*, 96th Cong., 1st sess., 1 March 1979, p. 191.

65. "Senate Panel Accepts Revised Extradition Treaty," *New York Times*, 13 June 1986, p. A7.

66. Weston, Falk, and D'Amato, *International Law and World Order*, p. 491.

67. Mickolus, *Transnational Terrorism*, pp. 325–326.

68. Weston, Falk, and D'Amato, *International Law and World Order*, p. 491.

69. Lewis A. Dunn, "Nuclear Proliferation and World Politics," in *American Defense Policy*, ed. John F. Reichart and Steven R. Sturm (Baltimore: The Johns Hopkins University Press, 1982), p. 452.

70. U.S. Congress, Senate, Committee on Foreign Relations, *International Terrorism: Hearings on S. 873*, 10 June 1981, p. 40.

71. Brian Michael Jenkins, "International Cooperation in Locating and Recovering Stolen Nuclear Materials," *Terrorism: An International Journal* 6, no. 4 (1983): 572.

72. Ibid.

73. Ibid, p. 573.

74. Ibid.

75. Ibid, p. 572.

76. U.S. Department of State, *International Terrorism*, p. 11.

77. U.S. Congress, House, Subcommittee on Arms Control, International Security and Science and on International Operations of the Committee on Foreign Affairs and the Subcommittee on Aviation of the Committee on Public Works and Transportation, *Joint Hearings: Impact of International Terrorism on Travel*, 19 February 1986, p. 31

78. Alona E. Evans and John E. Murphy, eds., *Legal Aspects of International Terrorism* (Lexington, Mass.: Lexington Books, 1978), pp. xv–xvi.

79. Ibid, p. 636.

80. Alexander, Browne, and Nanes, *Control of Terrorism*, p. 215.

81. U.S. Department of State, *Terrorism: Do Something, but What?* Department of State Bulletin (September 1979), p. 64.

82. (1) June 1980—Venice Economic Summit—Statement on the Taking of Diplomatic Hostages, (2) November 1980—North Atlantic Assembly Resolution on Terrorism, (3) December 1980—NATO Foreign Ministers—Declaration on Terrorism and U.S. Hostages in Iran, (4) 1983—Madrid Conference on Security and Cooperation in Europe—Provision on Terrorism, (5) May 1981—North Atlantic Council—Declaration on International Terrorism, (6) July 1981—Ottawa Economic Summit—Statement on Terrorism, (7) June 1984—London Economic Summit—Declaration on Terrorism and (8) December 1984—North Atlantic Council of Ministers' Final Communique.

83. U.S. Congress, Senate, Committee on Foreign Relations, *International Terrorism: Hearings on S. 873*, 10 June 1981, p. 90.

84. "A Summit of Substance," *Time* (May 19, 1986), pp. 15–16.

85. U.S. Congress, House, Subcommittee on Arms Control, International Security and Science and on International Operations of the Committee on Foreign Affairs and the Subcommittee on Aviation of the Committee on Public Works and Transportation, *Joint Hearings: Impact of International Terrorism on Travel*, 19 February 1986, p. 13.

86. U.S. Congress, House, Subcommittee on International Operations of the Committee on Foreign Affairs, *Aftermath of the Achille Lauro Incident: Hearings on H. Con. Res. 228*, 99th Cong., 1st sess., 30 October 1985, p. 22.

87. Interview, Kevin McConnell, International Relations Officer of the Department of State's Office for Combatting Terrorism, October 14, 1983.

88. U.S. Congress, House, Subcommittee on International Operations of the Committee on Foreign Affairs, *Aftermath of the Achille Lauro Incident*, 30 October 1985, p. 17.

89. U.S. Department of State, *International Terrorism: Current Trends and the U.S. Response*, Bureau of Public Affairs Circular no. 706 (Washington, D.C.: U.S. Department of State, Bureau of Public Affairs, Office of Communications, May 1985), p. 7.

90. "U.S. Quits Nicaragua Court Case: Administration Says Proceedings Became Propaganda Forum," *The Washington Post*, 19 February 1985, p. A1.

91. John F. Murphy, "State Self-Help and Problems of Public International Law," in *Legal Aspects of International Law*, eds. Alona E. Evans and John E. Murphy (Lexington, Mass.: Lexington Books, 1978), p. 564.

92. Ibid, p. 555.

93. Ibid, pp. 554–556.

94. Ibid, p. 557.

95. Ibid, p. 565.

8
U.S. Policy: Past, Present and Future

From the late 1960s until the fall of 1972, the U.S. antiterrorist program relied heavily on the use of international law and organizations. International terrorism was seen by the United States, and many other nations, as a secondary foreign policy issue.

However, the tragic events of the Munich Olympic Games in 1972 altered many nations' views of terrorism. The total lack of awareness of the terrorist threat and the lack of antiterrorist capabilities were addressed by the members of the international community with varying degrees of success. The U.S. response to the Munich incident—the formulation of the Cabinet Committee to Combat Terrorism and its working group—represents the first and most significant American response to international terrorism. It represents the institutional foundation on which the U.S. antiterrorism policy was to be based.

There occurred during the mid–1970s the institutional expansion of the antiterrorist bureaucracy, with the assignment of 11 additional agencies and departments to the U.S. antiterrorist effort. However, this period also demonstrated institutional and policy weaknesses. The Carter administration addressed these problems by restructuring the command structure of the antiterrorist bureaucracy and by establishing Delta Force. However, the seizure of the American Embassy in Teheran and the tragic failure of Operation Eagle Claw on the desert sands of Iran once again called into question U.S. antiterrorist capabilities and helped defeat President Carter in his 1980 reelection effort.

The day of the hostages' release, January 21, 1981, President Reagan was inaugurated. So began a continuing campaign of harsh public rhetoric against international terrorism, which has been stressed as a primary foreign policy consideration for the 1980s. Led first by Secretary of State Alexander Haig and then by his successor, George Shultz, international terrorism has become an element of the Reagan administration's globalist foreign policy. The terrorism issue has also become a part of the administration's East–West perception of world affairs.

Despite all of its harsh rhetoric, the Reagan administration's approach has had no positive impact on the deterrence, prevention and suppression of international terrorism, nor has it created a greater degree of safety for Americans traveling and living abroad. The first two years of the current administration witnessed 658 terrorist incidents involving American citizens and property.[1] This represents the greatest two–year American involvement in international terrorist incidents since the gathering of statistical data on terrorist activity. The 1983 murder of more than 240 U.S. Marines in Lebanon at the hands of a lone terrorist, and preceding and succeeding events in the Middle East, including the raid on Libya and continued incarceration of a number of Americans by unknown terrorists and the Iran arms-for-hostages affair, demonstrate the unpreparedness of the United States to combat international terrorism properly.

The preceding chapters have outlined many of the weaknesses in the American approach to combatting terrorism. However, a number of problems with the U.S. response in general and the Reagan administration's in particular must be illustrated.

In addressing the problem of terrorist behavior, it is important to recognize the methods, goals and attitudes of terrorists. A major weakness in the American antiterrorism program, one that is not unique to the present administration, is the inability of top U.S. decision-makers to recognize the fact that terrorists have a different perception of rationality, life and use of violence as a form of political expression and behavior. A terrorist does not have the Western premium on life and is generally willing to sacrifice his own for the cause. The Carter administration's handling of the Iranian affair is illustrative of the lack of American understanding of the terrorist mentality. Theodore White stated that "right through until this day, there's been this American inability to understand the true fanaticism of this man [Khomeni], not moved by any sense of compassion, by any concern for laws, by any understanding of international tradition."[2]

In conjunction with the lack of understanding of the terrorist perception is the problem of the American handling of contingency planning and crisis management. The U.S. contingency-planning and crisis-management program "has been one of denial."[3] Robert Kupperman has outlined the problem of U.S. crisis-management and planning as one in which we "keep our heads in the sand."[4] The organizations involved in crisis management and planning are afraid that preparing for different types of incidents would in the end help terrorists by illustrating the different ways to strike.[5]

Finally, the Reagan administration's use of terrorism as a public relations tool and foreign policy lever against the Soviet Union is an improper use of the issue. There is evidence of Soviet Union support of some terrorist organizations. However, support should not be equated with command. The present administration's attempt at finding evidence of Soviet control of some terrorist movements has led to the politicalization of this issue. The consequences of the Reagan administration's politicalization of the issue of terrorism, although not harmful politically to President Reagan at home, has added to the difficulty of dealing with the Soviet Union on important issues.

Another negative aspect of the Reagan administration's attempt to link international terrorism with Soviet behavior is its impact on the development of international cooperation in combatting terrorism. As Brian Jenkins pointed out, the Reagan administration's policy approach precludes any possible chance of the Soviet Union supporting U.S. efforts within the international community to deal with terrorism.[6]

In addition, the Reagan administration has exaggerated the threat of international terrorism. From 1968 to the end of 1980, 3,700 people were killed as a result of terrorist activity.[7] However, in 1980 alone, an estimated 10,000 people were killed in El Salvador.[8] International terrorism is a problem, but it must be kept in perspective. The Reagan administration's making the issue a moral one, like that of President Carter's early human rights campaign, raises doubts about the effectiveness of such an approach. Seth P. Tillman pointed out that "evangelical moralism in its varied forms . . . tends to be unrewarding for certain fundamental reasons—of which the most important is its extension into realms in which we are unable or, as we sometimes find at the crucial moment, simply unwilling to apply our national power."[9]

On October 25, 1984, while appearing at the Park Avenue Synagogue in New York, Secretary of State Shultz in a tough, if not hostile, address called for public support in the use of military force to combat terrorism. Shultz's assertion that the "public must understand *before the fact* that there is the potential for the loss of life of some of our fighting men and the loss of life of some innocent people" raises troubling moral questions that are only reinforced by the raid on Libya.[10] The United States and other nations are today fighting a shadowy conflict with a number of terrorist organizations and their supporters. The United States must never lose sight of the fact, however, that playing by the terrorists' rules of no rules is not acceptable for a democracy and that, as outlined by Robert Osgood, "political realism unguided by moral purpose will be self–defeating and futile."[11]

Finally, the policy position called for by the so–called Shultz Doctrine leaves unanswered many relevant questions. The target of National Security Decision Directive (NSDD) 138 is terrorism supported by states. However, what exactly is state terrorism? What is the role of state responsibility for actions carried out within its territory? What if a government, such as Lebanon's, does not have the means to police its own territory? Is it responsible for the terrorism carried out by the PLO against Israel or the violence that was directed at the U.S. Marines? There are many forms of terrorism: revolutionary, transnational, war and sub–revolutionary. How are these forms of behavior going to be handled by the so–called Shultz Doctrine?

The United States is not adequately prepared to deal with international terrorism either psychologically or physically. The present administration has spoken of and taken some tough actions to combat terrorism and its supporters. Instead of enhancing American efforts at dealing with terrorism, however, the administration's actions may have placed the United States in a position in which only unilateral actions are possible. The Reagan administration entered office in 1981 stating that reciprocity would be a cornerstone of its foreign policy, mainly with the Soviet Union. However, the administration must recognize that reciprocity can be used by other states as well. If the Reagan administration seeks to deal with terrorism and its supporters with actions that are based on weak moral, political and legal grounds, it could lead to other states using the same type of actions, based on like justifications; an example is the Republic of South Africa's May 1986 raids on three African nations. In addition, U.S. behavior could undermine multilateral and bilateral efforts at dealing with terrorism. Other states could point to the U.S. behavior as state terrorism and much more threatening to international stability than the actions of a few individuals.

Furthermore, what constitutes a successful counterterrorist operation? The release of the Mayaguez, even with the needless death of many U.S. Marines, and the raid on Libya were hailed as successes. These acts are successes only in the minds of senior Ford and Reagan administration officials. The Mayaguez was released before the rescue operation was begun, and the positive effects of the raid on Libya are questionable and unfortunately led to the execution of American hostage Peter Kilbourn. The Senate's Select Committee on Intelligence's preliminary report on the Iran arms–for–hostages affair stated that "in the aftermath of [the raid on Libya], hostage Peter Kilbourn was killed by his captors, reportedly at the behest of Libyan leader Muammar [Khaddafi]."[12] The psychological needs of officials to be viewed as doing something in the face of a threat led to the death of many Marines and U.S. citizens and has driven U.S. foreign policy for an extended period. The macho attitude inherent in U.S. foreign policy in general and in the so–called Shultz Doctrine in particular must be tempered by the realities of international affairs and international terrorism.

What is further puzzling about the Reagan administration's antiterrorist stance is its condemning of the May 1986 South African raids on three African states in which African National Congress members were based. There is no substantive difference between U.S. actions against Libya and the South African raids. The administration's condemning of South Africa is hypocritical and demonstrates its lack of understanding of terrorism and what retaliatory strikes really are and how they can harm the prestige of a nation.

The means used by the United States in combatting terrorism should always be proportional to the desired ends and must be based on accepted norms of conduct. The means called for by NSDD 138 and actions like the raid on Libya and the Iran arms–for–hostages affair could well undermine U.S. political, military, economic and moral goals and interests. The words of Robert Kupperman and David Williamson, Jr. are insightful:

> In the final analysis, our greatest protection from attack is not violent preemption but substantive knowledge, imaginative planning and well–prepared government leadership. What we seldom recognize is that the image of a forewarned nation is itself a powerful shield against attack. We need to develop and organize our visible and invisible resources––and then exercise them to prove to the terrorists and their supporters that we are able and willing to defend ourselves without compromising our honor and our ideals. [13]

The Reagan administration's aggressive stance on terrorism and Secretary Shultz's call for even tougher measures must also be weighed in the light of the administration's own terrorist behavior, that is, the mining of Nicaraguan harbors and CIA manuals on assassination. As Kupperman and Williamson stated: "the notion that their terrorism is automatically immoral and that our own counterterrorism is automatically moral will not stand much scrutiny." [14]

The unfortunate conclusion concerning the U.S. approach to terrorism is that it is not coherent, if it exists at all. What does exist are components of possibly a very effective antiterrorism policy and program, such as the Anti-terrorist Assistance Program and the Federal Aviation Administration's airport security program. The confusion created by the Reagan administration's tough and aggressive behavior toward Libya on the one hand and its willingness on the other to trade arms to Iran for the release of three American hostages has left many both inside and outside the United States asking what is U.S. policy and who is in charge?

The unfortunate reality of international terrorism is that there are no solutions. The best that can be achieved is damage control and the formulation of an antiterrorist policy and program that demonstrates an awareness of the complex nature of international terrorism and the sobering realities associated with it. The formulation of a comprehensive U.S. foreign policy that recognizes the realities and complex nature of world affairs and uses a regional and issue–oriented approach is necessary. What is not useful is, in John Lewis Gaddis' words, the Reagan administration's "mono–dimensional approach to national security [which] reveals a tendency to define interests and threats in chiefly military terms, with little or no awareness of the political, economic or psychological components of strategy." [15] The United States has attempted to combat international terrorism by implementing a tough antiterrorist program backed by a massive array of assets. But terrorism will continue. As long as individuals, groups and even nations view certain political, economic and social institutions as illegitimate, unacceptable and immoral, terrorist behavior will continue as a form of political expression.

NOTES

1.   U.S. Department of State, *Patterns of International Terrorism: 1982* (Washington, D.C.: Office for Combatting Terrorism, September 1983), p. 2.

2.   Theodore H. White, *America in Search of Itself: The Making of the President, 1956–1980* (New York: Harper & Row, 1982), p. 15.

3.   Laurence Gonzales, "The Targeting of America: A Special Report on Terrorism," *Playboy* (May 1983): 171.

4.   Ibid., p. 178.

5.   Ibid., p. 180.

6.   Brian Michael Jenkins, "International Terrorism: Choosing the Right Target," *The Rand Corporation* (March 1981): 1–8 passim.

7.   U.S. Department of State, *The Impact of International Terrorism*, Department of State Bulletin (January 1982), p. 55.

8.   Editorial, "Reagantalk, Haigspeak," *The Nation* (14 February 1981), p. 166.

9.   Seth P. Tillman, *The United States in the Middle East: Interests and Obstacles* (Bloomington, Ind.: Indiana University Press, 1982), p. 47.

10.   "Officials Split on Shultz's Antiterrorism Speech," *The Washington Post*, 27 October 1984, p. A1.

11.   Robert Osgood, *Ideals and Self-Interest in America's Foreign Relations* (Chicago: University of Chicago Press, 1953), p. 451.

12.   U.S. Congress, Senate, Select Committee on Intelligence, *Report on Preliminary Inquiry: Iran Contra Affair*, 100th Cong., 1st sess., January 29, 1987, p. 25.

13.   "Let's Calm Down and Get Smart about Terrorism," *The Washington Post*, 2 December 1984, p. D4.

14.   Ibid.

15.   John Lewis Gaddis, "The Rise, Fall, and Future of Detente," *Foreign Affairs* 62 (Winter 1983–84): 372.

Appendix

Heads of the State Department's Antiterrorist Office: 1972–1987

The following material outlines the evolution of the State Department's antiterrorist office from the creation of the position of Special Assistant to the Secretary of State and Coordinator for Combatting Terrorism in 1972 to the development of the Office for Counter-terrorism and Emergency Planning in February 1984 to the creation of the position of Ambassador-at-Large for Counterterrorism in 1985. The following list gives the name, title, approximate year(s) in office and career specialty before entering office of those officials who headed the State Department's antiterrorist office.

1. *Ambassador Armin H. Meyer*, Special Assistant to Secretary of State and Coordinator for Combatting Terrorism, October 1972–July 1973, Middle Eastern and Asian Affairs.
2. *Ambassador Lewis Hoffacker*, Special Assistant to Secretary of State and Coordinator for Combatting Terrorism, July 1973–May 1975, Middle Eastern and African Affairs.
3. *Foreign Service Officer Robert A. Fearey*, Special Assistant to Secretary of State and Coordinator for Combatting Terrorism, May 1975–May 1976, Asian and Pacific Affairs.
4. *Foreign Service Officer John N. Gatch*, Acting Special Assistant to Secretary of State and Coordinator for Combatting Terrorism, May 1976–August 1976, Middle Eastern and African Affairs.
5. *Ambassador L. Douglas Heck*, Director of the Office for Combatting Terrorism, August 1976–September 1977, Near Eastern Affairs.
6. *Foreign Service Officer John E. Karkashian*, Acting Director of the Office for Combatting Terrorism, September 1977–December 1977, Inter-American Affairs.
7. *Ambassador Heyward Isham*, Director of the Office for Combatting Terrorism, December 1977–Fall 1978, Generalist.
8. *Ambassador Anthony C. E. Quainton*, Director of the Office for Combatting Terrorism, Fall 1978–Fall 1981, Asian Affairs.
9. *Foreign Service Officer Frank H. Perez*, Acting Director of the Office for Combatting Terrorism, Fall 1981–May 1982, Political–Military Affairs.
10. *Ambassador Robert M. Sayre*, Director of the Office for Combatting Terrorism (May 1982 to February 1984) and Director of the Office for Counter-terrorism and Emergency Planning, February 1984–October 1984, Inter-American Affairs.

11.   *Ambassador Robert B. Oakley*, Director of the Office for Counter-terrorism and Emergency Planning (October 1984 to Fall 1985) and Ambassador-at-Large for Counterterrorism, Fall 1985 to September 1986, African East Asian and Pacific Affairs.
12.   *Ambassador L. Paul Bremer III*, Ambassador-at-Large for Counterterrorism (September 1986 to present), Administrative and European Affairs.

Source: Compiled from numerous sources with the help of Rosemary Reed of the *State Department Magazine*, U.S. Department of State.

Selected Bibliography

BOOKS

Alexander, Yonah; Browne, Marjorie Ann; and Nanes, Allan S. *Control of Terrorism: International Documents.* New York: Crane, Russak & Company, 1979.

Alexander, Yonah; Carlton, David; and Wilkinson, Paul, eds. *Terrorism: Theory and Practice.* Boulder, Colo.: Westview Press, 1979.

Barnett, Frank R.; Tovar, B. Hugh; and Schultz, Richard H., eds. *Special Operations in U.S. Strategy.* Washington D.C.: National Defense University Press, 1984.

Beckwith, Col. Charlie A., USA (Ret.), and Knox, Donald. *Delta Force.* New York: Harcourt Brace Jovanovich, 1983.

Beres, Louis Rene. *Terrorism and Global Security: The Nuclear Threat.* Boulder, Colo.: Westview Press, 1979.

Christopher, Warren, et al. *American Hostages in Iran: The Conduct of a Crisis.* New Haven: Yale University Press, 1985.

Crenshaw, Martha, ed. *Terrorism, Legitimacy, and Power: The Consequences of Political Violence.* Middletown, Conn.: Wesleyan University Press, 1983.

Dobson, Christopher, and Payne, Ronald. *Counterattack: The West's Battle against the Terrorists.* New York: Facts on File, 1982.

Dobson, Christopher, and Payne, Ronald. *The Terrorists: Their weapons, Leaders and Tactics.* New York: Facts on File, 1982.

Evans, Alona E., and Murphy, John F., eds. *Legal Aspects of International Terrorism.* Lexington, Mass.: Lexington Books, 1978.

Evans, Ernest. *Calling a Truce to Terror: The American Response to International Terrorism.* Westport, Conn.: Greenwood Press, 1979.

Farrell, William Regis. *The U.S. Government Response to Terrorism: In Search of an Effective Strategy.* Boulder, Colo.: Westview Press, 1982.

Freedman, Lawrence Zelic and Alexander, Yonah, eds. *Perspectives on Terrorism.* Wilmington, Del.: Scholarly Resources, 1983.

Godson, Roy, ed. *Intelligence Requirements for the 1980s: Counter-Intelligence.* Washington, D.C.: National Strategy Information Center, 1980.

Gurr, Ted Robert. *Why Men Rebel.* Princeton, N.J.: Princeton University Press, 1970.

Herz, Martin F., ed. *Diplomats and Terrorists: What Works, What Doesn't: A Symposium.* Washington, D.C.: Institute for the Study of Diplomacy, School of Foreign Service, Georgetown University, 1982.

Kupperman, Robert H., and Taylor, William, Jr., eds. *Strategic Requirements for the Army to the Year 2000.* Lexington, Mass.: Lexington Books, 1984.

Kupperman, Robert H., and Trent, Darrell. *Terrorism: Threat, Reality, Response.* Stanford, Calif.: Hoover Institution Press, 1979.

Livingston, Marius H.; Kress, Lee Bruce; and Wanek, Marie G., eds. *International Terrorism in the Contemporary World.* Westport, Conn.: Greenwood Press, 1978.

Livingstone, Neil C. *The War against Terrorism.* Lexington, Mass.: Lexington Books, 1982.

Mickolus, Edward F. *Transnational Terrorism: A Chronology of Events, 1968–1979.* Westport, Conn.: Greenwood Press, 1980.

Montana, Patrick J., and Roukis, George S., eds. *Managing Terrorism: Strategies for the Corporate Executive.* Westport, Conn.: Quorum Books, 1983.

Motley, James B. *U.S. Strategy to Counter Domestic Political Terrorism.* Washington, D.C.: National Defense University Press, 1983.

Ryan, Paul B. *The Iranian Rescue Mission: Why It Failed.* Annapolis, Md.: Naval Institute Press, 1985.

Schemmer, Benjamin F. *The Raid.* New York: Harper & Row Publishers, 1976.

Schmid, Alex P. *Political Terrorism: A Research Guide to Concepts, Theories, Data Bases and Literature.* Amsterdam: SWIDOC, 1983.

Schultz, Richard H., Jr., and Sloan, Steven, eds. *Responding to the Terrorist Threat: Security and Crisis Management.* New York: Pergamon Press, 1980.

Sick, Gary. *All Fall Down: America's Tragic Encounter with Iran.* New York: Random House, 1985.

Taylor, William J., Jr., and Maaranen, Steve A., eds. *The Future of Conflict in the 1980s.* Lexington, Mass.: Lexington Books, 1982.

Wardlaw, Grant. *Political Terrorism: Theory, Tactics and Countermeasures.* New York: Cambridge University Press, 1982.

ARTICLES

Bell, J. Bowyer. "Trends on Terror: The Analysis of Political Violence." *World Politics* 24 (April 1977): 476–488.

Bell, Robert G. "The U.S. Response to Terrorism against International Civil Aviation." *Orbis* 19 (Winter 1976): 1326–1343.

Breemer, Jan S. "Offshore Energy Terrorism: Perspectives on a Problem." *Terrorism: An International Journal* 6, no. 3 (1983): 455–465.

Cohen, Sen. William S. (R–Maine). "A Defense Special Agency: Fix for a SOF Capability That Is Most Assuredly Broken." *Armed Forces Journal International* (January 1986): 38–45.

Daniel, Rep. Dan (D–Va.). "U.S. Special Operations: The Case for Sixth Service." *Armed Forces Journal International* (August 1985): 70–75.

Dugard, John. "International Terrorism: Problems of Definition." *International Affairs* (Great Britain) 50 (January 1974): 67–81.

Fromkin, David. "The Strategy of Terrorism." *Foreign Affairs* 53 (July 1975): 683–698.

Frook, John. "Why They're Called 'Suicide Jockeys.'" *Parade Magazine* (July 3, 1983): 10.

Gaddis, John Lewis. "The Rise, Fall, and Future of Detente." *Foreign Affairs* 62 (Winter 1983–84): 354–377.

Gazit, Schlomo. "Risk, Glory, and the Rescue Operation." *International Security* 6 (Winter 1981–82): 111–135.

Gonzales, Laurence. "The Targeting of America: A Special Report on Terrorism." *Playboy* (May 1983): 89–90, 92, 171–172, 174–180.

Hamrick, Lt. Col. Tom, U.S. Army (Ret.). "The Black Berets." *Army* (May 1977): 28–33.

Jenkins, Brian Michael. "International Cooperation in Locating and Recovering Stolen Nuclear Materials." *Terrorism: An International Journal* 6, no. 4 (1983): 561–575.

Jenkins, Brian Michael. "International Terrorism: Choosing the Right Target." *The Rand Corporation* (March 1981): 1–8.

Jenkins, Brian Michael. "International Terrorism: Trends and Potentialities." *Journal of International Affairs* 32 (Spring–Summer 1978): 115–124.

Kaplan, Abraham. "The Psychodynamics of Terrorism." *Terrorism: An International Journal* 1, nos. 3 and 4 (1978): 237–254.

Koch, Noel C. "Two Cases against a Sixth Service." *Armed Forces Journal International* (October 1985): 102–109.

Lynch, Edward A. "International Terrorism: The Search for a Policy." *Terrorism: An International Journal* 9, no. 1 (1987): 1–85.

McDonald, Ambassador John W., Jr. "The United Nations Convention Against the Taking of Hostages: The Inside Story." *Terrorism: An International Journal* 6, no. 4 (1983): 545–560.

Meyer, Deborah G. "Four Years Later: Desert One Revisited?" *Armed Forces Journal International* (August 1985): 26.

Meyer, Deborah G., and Schemmer, Benjamin F. "An Exclusive AFJ Interview with: Noel C. Koch, Principal Deputy Assistant Secretary of Defense for International Security Affairs." *Armed Forces Journal International* (March 1985): 36–52.

Meyer, Deborah G., and Schemmer, Benjamin F. "Congressional Pressure May Force Far More DOD Dollars for Special Ops." *Armed Forces Journal International* (April 1986): 20–22.

Morelli, Major General Donald R., U.S. Army (Ret.), and Ferguson, Major (P) Michael M., U.S. Army. "Low–Intensity Conflict: An Operational Perspective." *Military Review* (November 1984): 2–16.

Motley, Colonel James B., U.S. Army (Ret.). "Terrorist Warfare: A Reassessment." *Military Review* (June 1985): 45–57.

Odorizzi, Charles D. "SOF Reorganization: Everyone Has a Plan—Senate, House, and DOD." *Armed Forces Journal International* (September 1986): 17–18.

Pierre, Andrew J. "The Politics of International Terrorism." *Orbis* 19 (Winter 1976): 1251–1269.

Schultz, Richard. "Conceptualizing Political Terrorism: A Typology." *Journal of International Affairs* 32 (Spring–Summer 1978): 7–15.

Sloan, Stephen. "In Search of a Counterterrorism Doctrine." *Military Review* (January 1986): 44–48.

Summers, Colonel Harry G., Jr., U.S. Army. "Delta Force: America's Counterterrorist Unit and the Mission to Rescue the Hostages in Iran." *Military Review* (November 1983): 21–27.

Waghelstein, Colonel John D., U.S. Army. "Post–Vietnam Counterinsurgency Doctrine." *Military Review* (May 1985): 42–49.

Wilkinson, Paul. "Three Questions on Terrorism." *Government and Opposition* 8 (Summer 1973): 290–312.

GOVERNMENT DOCUMENTS

Report of the DOD Commission on Beirut International Airport Terrorist Act, October 23, 1983. Admiral Robert L. Long, USN (Ret.), chairman. Washington, D.C.: U.S. Government Printing Office, 1984.

Report of the Secretary of State's Advisory Panel on Overseas Security. Admiral Bobby Inman, USN (Ret.), chairman. Washington, D.C.: U.S. Department of State, June 1985.

U.S. Armed Services. *Joint Special Operations Agency (JSOA), Joint Manpower Program (JMP)—FY 1984: Approved,* 25 June 1984.

U.S. Congress. House. Committee on Appropriations. *Department of Defense Appropriation Bill, 1986: Report to Accompany H.R. 3629.* 99th Cong., 1st sess., 1985, H. Rept. 332.

U.S. Congress. House. Subcommittee on Arms Controls, International Security and Science and on International Operations of the Committee on Foreign Affairs. *International Terrorism: 1985: Hearings on H.R. 2822.* 99th Cong., 2d sess., 5, 21 March and 25 June 1985.

U.S. Congress. House. Subcommittee on Arms Control, International Security and Science and on International Operations of the Committee on Foreign Affairs and the Subcommittee on Aviation of the Committee on Public Works and Transportation. *Joint Hearings: Impact of International Terrorism on Travel.* 99th Cong., 2d sess., 19 February; 17, 22 April; and 15 May 1986.

U.S. Congress. House. Subcommittee on Civil and Constitutional Rights of the Committee on the Judiciary. *Federal Capabilities in Crisis Management and Terrorism.* 95th Cong., 2d sess., 16 August 1978.

U.S. Congress. House. Subcommittee on Civil and Constitutional Rights of the Committee on the Judiciary. *Federal Capabilities in Crisis Management and Terrorism.* 96th Cong., 2d sess., 19 May 1980.

U.S. Congress. House. Subcommittee on the Department of Defense of the Committee on Appropriations. *Department of Defense Appropriations for 1982, pt 6: Counterterrorism Programs* 97th Cong., 1st sess., 24 June 1981.

U.S. Congress. House. Subcommittee on the Department of Defense of the Committee on Appropriations. *Department of Defense Appropriations for 1986: Special Operations Forces.* 99th Cong., 1st sess., 7 May 1985.

U.S. Congress. House. Subcommittee on the Department of Defense of the Committee on Appropriations. *Department of Defense Appropriations for 1987: Special Operations Forces.* 99th Cong., 2d sess., 10 April 1986.

U.S. Congress. House. Subcommittee on International Operations of the Committee on Foreign Affairs. *Aftermath of the Achille Lauro Incident: Hearings on H. Con. Res. 228.* 99th Cong., 1st sess., 30 October and 6, 7 November 1985.

U.S. Congress. Senate. Committee on Foreign Relations. *International Terrorism: Hearings on S. 873.* 97th Cong., 1st sess., 10 June 1981.

U.S. Congress. Senate. Committee on Governmental Affairs. *An Act to Combat International Terrorism: Hearings on S. 2236.* 95th Cong., 2d sess., 23, 25, and 27 January; 22 February; and 23 March 1978.

U.S. Congress. Senate. Committee on Governmental Affairs. *Omnibus Antiterrorism Act of 1979: Hearings on S. 333.* 96th Cong., 1st sess., 30 March and 7 May 1979.

U.S. Congress. Senate. Subcommittee on Foreign Assistance of the Committee on Foreign Relations. *International Terrorism.* 95th Cong., 1st sess., 14 September 1977.

U.S. Department of State. *The Challenge of Terrorism: The 1980s.* Bureau of Public Affairs' Circular no. 230. Washington, D.C.: U.S. Department of State, Bureau of Public Affairs, Office of Public Communication, 1980.

U.S. Department of State. *Combatting International Terrorism.* Department of State Bulletin (June 1985).

U.S. Department of State. *Combatting Terrorism: American Policy and Organization.* Department of State Bulletin (August 1982).

U.S. Department of State. *Counterterrorism Policy.* Bureau of Public Affairs Circular no. 823. Washington, D.C.: U.S. Department of State, Bureau of Public Affairs, Office of Communications, April 1986.

U.S. Department of State. *International Terrorism.* Department of State Bulletin (August 1986).

U.S. Department of State. *International Terrorism: Current Trends and the U.S. Response.* Bureau of Public Affairs Circular no. 706. Washington, D.C.: U.S. Department of State, Bureau of Public Affairs, Office of Communications, May 1985.

U.S. Department of State. *Patterns of International Terrorism: 1982.* Washington, D.C.: U.S. Department of State, Office for Combatting Terrorism, September 1983.

U.S. Department of State. *President Nixon Establishes Cabinet Committee to Combat Terrorism.* Department of State Bulletin (October 23, 1972).

U.S. Department of State. *Realism, Strength, Negotiations: Key Foreign Policy Statements of the Reagan Administration.* Washington, D.C.: U.S. Department of State, Bureau of Public Affairs, May 1984.

U.S. Department of State. *Terrorism: Do Something, but What?* Department of State Bulletin (September 1979).

U.S. Department of State. *The U.S. Government Response to Terrorism: A Global Approach.* Department of State Bulletin (March 18, 1974).

U.S. Department of State. *A World Free of Violence.* Department of State Bulletin (October 16, 1972).

U.S. National Security Council. *The United States Government Antiterrorism Program: An Unclassified Summary Report.* Washington, D.C.: Executive Committee on Terrorism of the Special Coordination Committee of the National Security Council, June 1979.

U.S. President. Executive Order 12333. "United States Intelligence Activities." *Weekly Compilation of Presidential Documents* 17 (October–December 1981).

Index

About the Author

MARC A. CELMER works in private industry. He has a Master's degree from the School of International Service at American University in Washington, D.C.